# THE SCHOOL FOR SCANDAL

By Richard B. Sheridan

The poem is in Iambic pentameter. using rhyming couplets.

Sheridan elevates Mrs Crewe to the point where she seems 'too good to be true' she is not only physically beautiful. but her personality is also to be commended

Sheridan seems to feel negatively towards these people as we see him describe them derogniatory terms

A Digireads.com Book
Digireads.com Publishing
16212 Riggs Rd
Stilwell, KS, 66085

The School for Scandal
By Richard Brinsley Sheridan
ISBN: 1-4209-2715-9



Please visit *www.digireads.com*

## INTRODUCTION

ADDRESSED TO MRS. CREWE,
WITH THE COMEDY OF THE SCHOOL FOR SCANDAL

BY R. B. SHERIDAN, ESQ.

Tell me, ye prim adepts in Scandal's school,
Who rail by precept, and detract by rule,
Lives there no character, so tried, so known,
So deck'd with grace, and so unlike your own,
That even you assist her fame to raise,
Approve by envy, and by silence praise!—
Attend!—a model shall attract your view—
Daughters of calumny, I summon you!
You shall decide if this a portrait prove,
Or fond creation of the Muse and Love.—
Attend, ye virgin critics, shrewd and sage,
Ye matron censors of this childish age,
Whose peering eye and wrinkled front declare
A fixt antipathy to young and fair;
By cunning, cautious; or by nature, cold,
In maiden madness, virulently bold!—
Attend! ye skilled to coin the precious tale,
Creating proof, where innuendos fail!
Whose practised memories, cruelly exact,
Omit no circumstance, except the fact!—
Attend, all ye who boast,—or old or young,—
The living libel of a slanderous tongue!
So shall my theme as far contrasted be,
As saints by fiends, or hymns by calumny.
Come, gentle Amoret (for 'neath that name,
In worthier verse is sung thy beauty's fame);
Come—for but thee who seeks the Muse? and while
Celestial blushes check thy conscious smile,
With timid grace, and hesitating eye,
The perfect model, which I boast, supply:—
Vain Muse! couldst thou the humblest sketch create
Of her, or slightest charm couldst imitate—
Could thy blest strain in kindred colours trace
The faintest wonder of her form and face—

Poets would study the immortal line,
And *Reynolds* own *his* art subdued by thine;
That art, which well might added lustre give
To Nature's best and Heaven's superlative:
On *Granby's* cheek might bid new glories rise,
Or point a purer beam from *Devon's* eyes!
Hard is the task to shape that beauty's praise,
Whose judgment scorns the homage flattery pays!
But praising Amoret we cannot err,
No tongue o'ervalues Heaven, or flatters her!
Yet she, by Fate's perverseness—she alone
Would doubt our truth, nor deem such praise her own!
Adorning Fashion, unadorn'd by dress,
Simple from taste, and not from carelessness;
Discreet in gesture, in deportment mild,
Not stiff with prudence, nor uncouthly wild:
No state has *Amoret!* no studied mien;
She frowns no *goddess*, and she moves no *queen.*
The softer charm that in her manner lies
Is framed to captivate, yet not surprise;
It justly suits th' expression of her face,—
'Tis less than dignity, and more than grace!
On her pure cheek the native hue is such,
That, form'd by Heav'n to be admired so much,
The hand divine, with a less partial care,
Might well have fix'd a fainter crimson there,
And bade the gentle inmate of her breast,—
Inshrined Modesty!—supply the rest.
But who the peril of her lips shall paint?
Strip them of smiles—still, still all words are faint!
But moving Love himself appears to teach
Their action, though denied to rule her speech;
And thou who seest her speak and dost not hear,
Mourn not her distant accents 'scape thine ear;
Viewing those lips, thou still may'st make pretence
To judge of what she says, and swear 'tis sense:
Cloth'd with such grace, with such expression fraught,
They move in meaning, and they pause in thought!
But dost thou farther watch, with charm'd surprise,
The mild irresolution of her eyes,
Curious to mark how frequent they repose,
In brief eclipse and momentary close—

Ah! seest thou not an ambush'd Cupid there,
Too tim'rous of his charge, with jealous care
Veils and unveils those beams of heav'nly light,
Too full, too fatal else, for mortal sight?
Nor yet, such pleasing vengeance fond to meet,
In pard'ning dimples hope a safe retreat.
What though her peaceful breast should ne'er allow
Subduing frowns to arm her altered brow,
By Love, I swear, and by his gentle wiles,
More fatal still the mercy of her smiles!
Thus lovely, thus adorn'd, possessing all
Of bright or fair that can to woman fall,
The height of vanity might well be thought
Prerogative in her, and Nature's fault.
Yet gentle *Amoret*, in mind supreme
As well as charms, rejects the vainer theme;
And, half mistrustful of her beauty's store,
She barbs with wit those darts too keen before:—
Read in all knowledge that her sex should reach,
Though *Greville*, or the *muse*, should deign to teach,
Fond to improve, nor tim'rous to discern
How far it is a woman's grace to learn;
In *Millar's* dialect she would not prove
Apollo's priestess, but Apollo's love,
Graced by those signs which truth delights to own,
The timid blush, and mild submitted tone:
Whate'er she says, though sense appear throughout,
Displays the tender hue of female doubt;
Deck'd with that charm, how lovely wit appears,
How graceful *science*, when that robe she wears!
Such too her talents, and her bent of mind,
As speak a sprightly heart by thought refined:
A taste for mirth, by contemplation school'd,
A turn for ridicule, by candour ruled,
A scorn of folly, which she tries to hide;
An awe of talent, which she owns with pride!
Peace, idle Muse! no more thy strain prolong,
But yield a theme thy warmest praises wrong;
Just to her merit, though thou canst not raise
Thy feeble verse, behold th' acknowledged praise
Has spread conviction through the envious train,
And cast a fatal gloom o'er Scandal's reign!

And lo! each pallid hag, with blister'd tongue,
Mutters assent to all thy zeal has sung—
Owns all the colours just—the outline true;
Thee my inspirer, and my *model—Crewe!*

**DRAMATIS PERSONAE**

SIR PETER TEAZLE
SIR OLIVER SURFACE
YOUNG SURFACE
CHARLES (his Brother)
CRABTREE
SIR BENJAMIN BACKBITE
ROWLEY
SPUNGE
MOSES
SNAKE
CARELESS—and other companions to CHARLES

LADY TEAZLE
MARIA
LADY SNEERWELL
MRS. CANDOUR
MISS VERJUICE

## PROLOGUE

WRITTEN BY MR. GARRICK

A school for Scandal! tell me, I beseech you,
Needs there a school this modish art to teach you?
No need of lessons now, the knowing think;
We might as well be taught to eat and drink.
Caused by a dearth of scandal, should the vapours
Distress our fair ones—let them read the papers;
Their powerful mixtures such disorders hit;
Crave what you will—there's *quantum sufficit*.
"Lord!" cries my Lady Wormwood (who loves tattle,
And puts much salt and pepper in her prattle),
Just risen at noon, all night at cards when threshing
Strong tea and scandal—"Bless me, how refreshing!
Give me the papers, Lisp—how bold and free! [Sips.]
*Last night Lord L.* [Sips] *was caught with Lady D.*
For aching heads what charming sal volatile! [Sips.]
*If Mrs. B. will still continue flirting,*
*We hope she'll* draw, *or we'll* undraw *the curtain.*
Fine satire, poz—in public all abuse it,
But, by ourselves [Sips], our praise we can't refuse it.
Now, Lisp, read you—there, at that dash and star:"
"Yes, ma'am—*A certain lord had best beware,*
*Who lives not twenty miles from Grosvenor Square*;
*For should he Lady W. find willing,*
*Wormwood is bitter*"——"Oh! that's me! the villain!
Throw it behind the fire, and never more
Let that vile paper come within my door."
Thus at our friends we laugh, who feel the dart;
To reach our feelings, we ourselves must smart.
Is our young bard so young, to think that he
Can stop the full spring-tide of calumny?
Knows he the world so little, and its trade?
Alas! the devil's sooner raised than laid.
So strong, so swift, the monster there's no gagging:
Cut Scandal's head off, still the tongue is wagging.
Proud of your smiles once lavishly bestow'd,
Again our young Don Quixote takes the road;
To show his gratitude he draws his pen,

And seeks his hydra, Scandal, in his den.
For your applause all perils he would through—
He'll fight—that's write—a cavalliero true,
Till every drop of blood—that's ink—is spilt for you.

Garrick is slightly sardonic when it comes to Sheridan and the play

He wonders whether Sheridan seriously thinks he will be able to stop Scandal-mongering through the play and suggests that it is more important to him that the audience applaud his efforts— and enjoy his play- despite its ineffectiveness at stopping scandal-mongering

# ACT I

## SCENE I

LADY SNEERWELL'S Dressing-room

[LADY SNEERWELL discovered at her toilet; SNAKE drinking chocolate.]

LADY SNEERWELL: The paragraphs, you say, Mr. Snake, were all inserted?

SNAKE. They were, madam; and, as I copied them myself in a feigned hand, there can be no suspicion whence they came.

LADY SNEERWELL. Did you circulate the report of Lady Brittle's intrigue with Captain Boastall?

SNAKE. That's in as fine a train as your ladyship could wish. In the common course of things, I think it must reach Mrs. Clackitt's ears within four-and-twenty hours; and then, you know, the business is as good as done.

LADY SNEERWELL. Why, truly, Mrs. Clackitt has a very pretty talent, and a great deal of industry.

SNAKE. True, madam, and has been tolerably successful in her day. To my knowledge, she has been the cause of six matches being broken off, and three sons being disinherited; of four forced elopements, and as many close confinements; nine separate maintenances, and two divorces. Nay, I have more than once traced her causing a *tête-à-tête* in the "Town and County Magazine," when the parties, perhaps, had never seen each other's face before in the course of their lives.

LADY SNEERWELL. She certainly has talents, but her manner is gross.

SNAKE. 'Tis very true. She generally designs well, has a free tongue and a bold invention; but her colouring is too dark, and her outlines often extravagant. She wants that delicacy of tint, and mellowness of sneer, which distinguish your ladyship's scandal.

LADY SNEERWELL. You are partial, Snake.

SNAKE. Not in the least; everybody allows that Lady Sneerwell can do more with a word or look than many can with the most laboured detail, even when they happen to have a little truth on their side to support it.

LADY SNEERWELL. Yes, my dear Snake; and I am no hypocrite to deny the satisfaction I reap from the success of my efforts. Wounded myself, in the early part of my life, by the envenomed tongue of slander, I confess I have since known no pleasure equal to the reducing others to the level of my own reputation.

SNAKE. Nothing can be more natural. But, Lady Sneerwell, there is one affair in which you have lately employed me, wherein, I confess, I am at a loss to guess your motives.

LADY SNEERWELL. I conceive you mean with respect to my neighbour, Sir Peter Teazle, and his family?

SNAKE. I do. Here are two young men, to whom Sir Peter has acted as a kind of guardian since their father's death; the eldest possessing the most amiable character, and universally well spoken of—the youngest, the most dissipated and extravagant young fellow in the kingdom, without friends or character; the former an avowed admirer of your ladyship, and apparently your favourite; the latter attached to Maria, Sir Peter's ward, and confessedly beloved by her. Now, on the face of these circumstances, it is utterly unaccountable to me, why you, the widow of a city knight, with a good jointure, should not close with the passion of a man of such character and expectations as Mr. Surface; and more so why you should be so uncommonly earnest to destroy the mutual attachment subsisting between his brother Charles and Maria.

LADY SNEERWELL. Then, at once to unravel this mystery, I must inform you that love has no share whatever in the intercourse between Mr. Surface and me.

SNAKE. No!

LADY SNEERWELL. His real attachment is to Maria, or her fortune; but, finding in his brother a favoured rival, he has been obliged to mask his pretensions, and profit by my assistance.

SNAKE. Yet still I am more puzzled why you should interest yourself in his success.

LADY SNEERWELL. Heavens! how dull you are! Cannot you surmise the weakness which I hitherto, through shame, have concealed even from you? Must I confess that Charles—that libertine, that extravagant, that bankrupt in fortune and reputation—that he it is for whom I am thus anxious and malicious, and to gain whom I would sacrifice every thing?

SNAKE. Now, indeed, your conduct appears consistent: but how came you and Mr. Surface so confidential?

LADY SNEERWELL. For our mutual interest. I have found him out a long time since. I know him to be artful, selfish, and malicious—in short, a sentimental knave; while with Sir Peter, and indeed with all his acquaintance, he passes for a youthful miracle of prudence, good sense, and benevolence.

SNAKE. Yes; yet Sir Peter vows he has not his equal in England; and, above all, he praises him as a man of sentiment.

LADY SNEERWELL. True; and with the assistance of his sentiment and hypocrisy he has brought Sir Peter entirely into his interest with regard to Maria; while poor Charles has no friend in the house—though, I fear, he has a powerful one in Maria's heart, against whom we must direct our schemes.

[Enter SERVANT.]

SERVANT. Mr. Surface.

LADY SNEERWELL. Show him up. [Exit Servant.] He generally calls about this time. I don't wonder at people giving him to me for a lover.

[Enter JOSEPH SURFACE.]

JOSEPH. My dear Lady Sneerwell, how do you do today? Mr. Snake, your most obedient.

LADY SNEERWELL. Snake has just been rallying me on our mutual attachment, but I have informed him of our real views. You know how useful he has been to us; and, believe me, the confidence is not ill-placed.

JOSEPH. Madam, it is impossible for me to suspect a man of Mr. Snake's sensibility and discernment.

LADY SNEERWELL. Well, well, no compliments now; but tell me when you saw your mistress, Maria—or, what is more material to me, your brother.

JOSEPH. I have not seen either since I left you; but I can inform you that they never meet. Some of your stories have taken a good effect on Maria.

LADY SNEERWELL. Ah, my dear Snake! the merit of this belongs to you. But do your brother's distresses increase?

JOSEPH. Every hour. I am told he has had another execution in the house yesterday. In short, his dissipation and extravagance exceed any thing I have ever heard of.

LADY SNEERWELL. Poor Charles!

JOSEPH. True, madam; notwithstanding his vices, one can't help feeling for him. Poor Charles! I'm sure I wish it were in my power to be of any essential service to him; for the man who does not share in the distresses of a brother, even though merited by his own misconduct, deserves—

LADY SNEERWELL. O Lud! you are going to be moral, and forget that you are among friends.

JOSEPH. Egad, that's true! I'll keep that sentiment till I see Sir Peter. However, it is certainly a charity to rescue Maria from such a libertine, who if he is to be reclaimed, can be so only by a person of your ladyship's superior accomplishments and understanding.

SNAKE. I believe, Lady Sneerwell, here's company coming: I'll go and copy the letter I mentioned to you. Mr. Surface, your most obedient.

JOSEPH. Sir, your very devoted.—[Exit SNAKE.] Lady Sneerwell, I am very sorry you have put any farther confidence in that fellow.

LADY SNEERWELL. Why so?

JOSEPH. I have lately detected him in frequent conference with old Rowley, who was formerly my father's steward, and has never, you know, been a friend of mine.

LADY SNEERWELL. And do you think he would betray us?

JOSEPH. Nothing more likely; take my word for't Lady Sneerwell, that fellow hasn't virtue enough to be faithful even to his own villainy. Ah, Maria!

[Enter MARIA.]

LADY SNEERWELL. Maria, my dear, how do you do? What's the matter?

MARIA. Oh! there's that disagreeable lover of mine, Sir Benjamin Backbite, has just called at my guardian's, with his odious uncle, Crabtree; so I slipped out, and ran hither to avoid them.

LADY SNEERWELL. Is that all?

JOSEPH. If my brother Charles had been of the party, madam, perhaps you would not have been so much alarmed.

LADY SNEERWELL. Nay, now you are severe; for I dare swear the truth of the matter is, Maria heard you were here. But, my dear, what has Sir Benjamin done, that you should avoid him so?

MARIA. Oh, he has done nothing—but 'tis for what he has said: his conversation is a perpetual libel on all his acquaintance.

JOSEPH. Ay, and the worst of it is, there is no advantage in not knowing him; for he'll abuse a stranger just as soon as his best friend: and his uncle's as bad.

LADY SNEERWELL. Nay, but we should make allowance; Sir Benjamin is a wit and a poet.

MARIA. For my part, I own, madam, wit loses its respect with me, when I see it in company with malice. What do you think, Mr. Surface?

JOSEPH. Certainly, madam; to smile at the jest which plants a thorn in another's breast is to become a principal in the mischief.

LADY SNEERWELL. Pshaw! there's no possibility of being witty without a little ill nature: the malice of a good thing is the barb that makes it stick. What's your opinion, Mr. Surface?

JOSEPH. To be sure, madam; that conversation, where the spirit of raillery is suppressed, will ever appear tedious and insipid.

MARIA. Well, I'll not debate how far scandal may be allowable; but in a man, I am sure, it is always contemptible. We have pride, envy, rivalship, and a thousand motives to depreciate each other; but the male slanderer must have the cowardice of a woman before he can traduce one.

[Re-enter SERVANT.]

SERVANT. Madam, Mrs. Candour is below, and, if your ladyship's at leisure, will leave her carriage.

LADY SNEERWELL. Beg her to walk in.—[Exit SERVANT.] Now, Maria, here is a character to your taste; for, though Mrs. Candour is a little talkative, every body allows her to be the best natured and best sort of woman.

MARIA. Yes, with a very gross affectation of good nature and benevolence, she does more mischief than the direct malice of old Crabtree.

JOSEPH. I' faith that's true, Lady Sneerwell: whenever I hear the current running against the characters of my friends, I never think them in such danger as when Candour undertakes their defence.

LADY SNEERWELL. Hush!—here she is!

[Enter MRS. CANDOUR.]

MRS. CANDOUR. My dear Lady Sneerwell, how have you been this century!—Mr. Surface, what news do you hear?—though indeed it is no matter, for I think one hears nothing else but scandal.

JOSEPH. Just so, indeed, ma'am.

MRS. CANDOUR. Oh, Maria! child,—what, is the whole affair off between you and Charles? His extravagance, I presume—the town talks of nothing else.

MARIA. I am very sorry, ma'am, the town has so little to do.

MRS. CANDOUR. True, true, child: but there's no stopping people's tongues. I own I was hurt to hear it, as I indeed was to learn, from the same quarter, that your guardian, Sir Peter, and Lady Teazle have not agreed lately as well as could be wished.

MARIA. 'Tis strangely impertinent for people to busy themselves so.

MRS. CANDOUR. Very true, child: but what's to be done? People will talk—there's no preventing it. Why, it was but yesterday I was told that Miss Gadabout had eloped with Sir Filigree Flirt. But, Lord! there's no minding what one hears; though, to be sure, I had this from very good authority.

MARIA. Such reports are highly scandalous.

MRS. CANDOUR. So they are, child—shameful, shameful! But the world is so censorious, no character escapes. Lord, now who would have suspected your friend, Miss Prim, of an indiscretion? Yet such is the ill nature of people, that they say her uncle stopped her last week, just as she was stepping into the York Mail with her dancing-master.

MARIA. I'll answer for't there are no grounds for that report.

MRS. CANDOUR. Ah, no foundation in the world, I dare swear; no more, probably, than for the story circulated last month, of Mrs. Festino's affair with Colonel Cassino—though, to be sure, that matter was never rightly cleared up.

JOSEPH. The license of invention some people take is monstrous indeed.

MARIA. 'Tis so; but, in my opinion, those who report such things are equally culpable.

MRS. CANDOUR. To be sure they are; tale-bearers are as bad as the tale-makers—'tis an old observation, and a very true one: but what's to be done, as I said before? how will you prevent people from talking? To-day, Mrs. Clackitt assured me, Mr. and Mrs. Honeymoon were at last become mere man and wife, like the rest of their acquaintance. She likewise hinted that a certain widow, in the next street, had got rid of her dropsy and recovered her shape in a most surprising manner. And at the same time Miss Tattle, who was by, affirmed that Lord Buffalo had discovered his lady at a house of no extraordinary fame; and that Sir Harry Bouquet and Tom Saunter were to measure swords on a similar provocation.

But, Lord, do you think I would report these things! No, no! tale-bearers, as I said before, are just as bad as the tale-makers.

JOSEPH. Ah! Mrs. Candour, if every body had your forbearance and good nature!

MRS. CANDOUR. I confess, Mr. Surface, I cannot bear to hear people attacked behind their backs; and when ugly circumstances come out against our acquaintance, I own I always love to think the best. By the by, I hope 'tis not true that your brother is absolutely ruined?

JOSEPH. I am afraid his circumstances are very bad indeed, ma'am.

MRS. CANDOUR. Ah! I heard so—but you must tell him to keep up his spirits; every body almost is in the same way: Lord Spindle, Sir Thomas Splint, Captain Quinze, and Mr. Nickit—all up, I hear, within this week; so, if Charles is undone, he'll find half his acquaintance ruined too, and that, you know, is a consolation.

JOSEPH. Doubtless, ma'am—a very great one.

[Re-enter SERVANT.]

SERVANT. Mr. Crabtree and Sir Benjamin Backbite. [Exit.]

LADY SNEERWELL. So, Maria, you see your lover pursues you; positively you shan't escape.

[Enter CRABTREE and SIR BENJAMIN BACKBITE.]

CRABTREE. Lady Sneerwell, I kiss your hand. Mrs. Candour, I don't believe you are acquainted with my nephew, Sir Benjamin Backbite? Egad, ma'am he has a pretty wit, and is a pretty poet too. Isn't he, Lady Sneerwell?

SIR BENJAMIN. Oh, fie, uncle!

CRABTREE. Nay, egad, it's true; I back him at a rebus or a charade against the best rhymer in the kingdom. Has your ladyship heard the epigram he wrote last week on Lady Frizzle's feather catching fire?—Do, Benjamin, repeat it, or the charade you made last night extempore at Mrs. Drowzie's conversazione. Come, now, your first is the name of a fish, your second a great naval commander, and—

SIR BENJAMIN. Uncle, now—pr'thee—

CRABTREE. I'faith, ma'am 'twould surprise you to hear how ready he is at all these sorts of things.

LADY SNEERWELL. I wonder, Sir Benjamin, you never publish any thing.

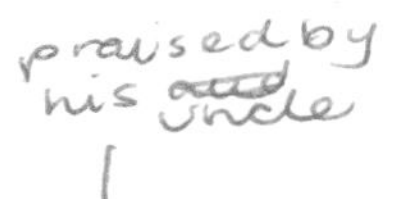



SIR BENJAMIN. To say truth, ma'am, 'tis very vulgar to print; and as my little productions are mostly satires and lampoons on particular people, I find they circulate more by giving copies in confidence to the friends of the parties. However, I have some love elegies, which, when favoured with this lady's smiles, I mean to give the public. [Pointing to MARIA.]

CRABTREE. [To MARIA.] 'Fore heaven, ma'am, they'll immortalize you!—you will be handed down to posterity, like Petrarch's Laura, or Waller's Sacharissa.

SIR BENJAMIN. [To MARIA.] Yes, madam, I think you will like them, when you shall see them on a beautiful quarto page, where a neat rivulet of text shall meander through a meadow of margin. 'Fore Gad they will be the most elegant things of their kind!

CRABTREE. But, ladies, that's true—have you heard the news?

MRS. CANDOUR. What, sir, do you mean the report of—

CRABTREE. No, ma'am, that's not it.—Miss Nicely is going to be married to her own footman.

MRS. CANDOUR. Impossible!

CRABTREE. Ask Sir Benjamin.

SIR BENJAMIN. 'Tis very true, ma'am: every thing is fixed, and the wedding liveries bespoke.

CRABTREE. Yes—and they do say there were pressing reasons for it.

LADY SNEERWELL. Why, I have heard something of this before.

MRS. CANDOUR. It can't be—and I wonder any one should believe such a story of so prudent a lady as Miss Nicely.

SIR BENJAMIN. O Lud! ma'am, that's the very reason 'twas believed at once. She has always been so cautious and so reserved, that every body was sure there was some reason for it at bottom.

MRS. CANDOUR. Why, to be sure, a tale of scandal is as fatal to the credit of a prudent lady of her stamp as a fever is generally to those of the strongest constitutions. But there is a sort of puny sickly reputation, that is always ailing, yet will outlive the robuster characters of a hundred prudes.

SIR BENJAMIN. True, madam, there are valetudinarians in reputation as well as constitution, who, being conscious of their weak part, avoid the least breath of air, and supply their want of stamina by care and circumspection.

MRS. CANDOUR. Well, but this may be all a mistake. You know, Sir Benjamin, very trifling circumstances often give rise to the most injurious tales.

CRABTREE. That they do, I'll be sworn, ma'am. Did you ever hear how Miss Piper came to lose her lover and her character last summer at Tunbridge?—Sir Benjamin, you remember it?

SIR BENJAMIN. Oh, to be sure!—the most whimsical circumstance.

LADY SNEERWELL. How was it, pray?

CRABTREE. Why, one evening, at Mrs. Ponto's assembly, the conversation happened to turn on the breeding Nova Scotia sheep in this country. Says a young lady in company, "I have known instances of it; for Miss Letitia Piper, a first cousin of mine, had a Nova Scotia sheep that produced her twins." "What!" cries the Lady Dowager Dundizzy (who you know is as deaf as a post), "has Miss Piper had twins?" This mistake, as you may imagine, threw the whole company into a fit of laughter. However, 'twas the next morning everywhere reported, and in a few days believed by the whole town, that Miss Letitia Piper had actually been brought to bed of a fine boy and a girl: and in less than a week there were some people who could name the father, and the farm-house where the babies were put to nurse.

LADY SNEERWELL. Strange, indeed!

CRABTREE. Matter of fact, I assure you. O Lud! Mr. Surface, pray is it true that your uncle, Sir Oliver, is coming home?

JOSEPH. Not that I know of, indeed, sir.

CRABTREE. He has been in the East Indies a long time. You can scarcely remember him, I believe? Sad comfort, whenever he returns, to hear how your brother has gone on!

JOSEPH. Charles has been imprudent, sir, to be sure; but I hope no busy people have already prejudiced Sir Oliver against him. He may reform.

SIR BENJAMIN. To be sure he may: for my part, I never believed him to be so utterly void of principle as people say; and, though he has lost all his friends, I am told nobody is better spoken of by the Jews.

CRABTREE. That's true, egad, nephew. If the Old Jewry was a ward, I believe Charles would be an alderman: no man more popular there, 'fore Gad! I hear he pays as many annuities as the Irish tontine; and that, whenever he is sick, they have prayers for the recovery of his health in all the synagogues.

SIR BENJAMIN. Yet no man lives in greater splendour. They tell me, when he entertains his friends he will sit down to dinner with a dozen of his own securities; have a score of tradesmen waiting in the antechamber, and an officer behind every guest's chair.

JOSEPH. This may be entertainment to you, gentlemen, but you pay very little regard to the feelings of a brother.

MARIA. [Aside.] Their malice is intolerable!—[Aloud.] Lady Sneerwell, I must wish you a good morning: I'm not very well. [Exit.]

MRS. CANDOUR. O dear! she changes colour very much.

LADY SNEERWELL. Do, Mrs. Candour, follow her: she may want your assistance.

MRS. CANDOUR. That I will, with all my soul, ma'am.—Poor dear girl, who knows what her situation may be! [Exit.]

LADY SNEERWELL. 'Twas nothing but that she could not bear to hear Charles reflected on, notwithstanding their difference.

SIR BENJAMIN. The young lady's *penchant* is obvious.

CRABTREE. But, Benjamin, you must not give up the pursuit for that: follow her, and put her into good humour. Repeat her some of your own verses. Come, I'll assist you.

SIR BENJAMIN. Mr. Surface, I did not mean to hurt you; but depend on't your brother is utterly undone.

CRABTREE. O Lud, ay! undone as ever man was—can't raise a guinea!

SIR BENJAMIN. And everything sold, I'm told, that was movable.

CRABTREE. I have seen one that was at his house. Not a thing left but some empty bottles that were overlooked, and the family pictures, which I believe are framed in the wainscots.

SIR BENJAMIN. And I'm very sorry also to hear some bad stories against him. [Going.]

CRABTREE. Oh, he has done many mean things, that's certain.

SIR BENJAMIN. But, however, as he's your brother— [Going.]

CRABTREE. We'll tell you all another opportunity. [Exeunt CRABTREE and SIR BENJAMIN.]

LADY SNEERWELL. Ha! ha! 'tis very hard for them to leave a subject they have not quite run down.

JOSEPH. And I believe the abuse was no more acceptable to your ladyship than Maria.

LADY SNEERWELL. I doubt her affections are farther engaged than we imagine. But the family are to be here this evening, so you may as well dine where you are, and we shall have an opportunity of observing farther; in the meantime, I'll go and plot mischief, and you shall study sentiment. [Exeunt.]

## SCENE II

### A Room in SIR PETER TEAZLE'S House

[Enter SIR PETER TEAZLE.]

SIR PETER. When an old bachelor marries a young wife, what is he to expect? 'Tis now six months since Lady Teazle made me the happiest of men—and I have been the most miserable dog ever since! We tiffed a little going to church, and fairly quarrelled before the bell had done ringing. I was more than once nearly choked with gall during the honeymoon, and had lost all comfort in life before my friends had done wishing me joy. Yet I chose with caution—a girl bred wholly in the country, who never knew luxury beyond one silk gown, nor dissipation above the annual gala of a race ball. Yet she now plays her part in all the extravagant fopperies of fashion and the town, with as ready a grace as if she never had seen a bush or a grass-plot out of Grosvenor Square! I am sneered at by all my acquaintance, and paragraphed in the newspapers. She dissipates my fortune, and contradicts all my humours; yet the worst of it is, I doubt I love her, or I should never bear all this. However, I'll never be weak enough to own it.

[Enter ROWLEY.]

ROWLEY. Oh! Sir Peter, your servant: how is it with you, sir?

SIR PETER. Very bad, Master Rowley, very bad. I meet with nothing but crosses and vexations.

ROWLEY. What can have happened since yesterday?

SIR PETER. A good question to a married man!

ROWLEY. Nay, I'm sure, Sir Peter, your lady can't be the cause of your uneasiness.

SIR PETER. Why, has any body told you she was dead?

ROWLEY. Come, come, Sir Peter, you love her, notwithstanding your tempers don't exactly agree.

SIR PETER. But the fault is entirely hers, Master Rowley. I am, myself, the sweetest-tempered man alive, and hate a teasing temper; and so I tell her a hundred times a day.

ROWLEY. Indeed!

SIR PETER. Ay; and what is very extraordinary, in all our disputes she is always in the wrong! But Lady Sneerwell, and the set she meets at her house, encourage the perverseness of her disposition. Then, to complete my vexation, Maria, my ward, whom I ought to have the power of a father over, is determined to turn rebel too, and absolutely refuses the man whom I have long resolved on for her husband; meaning, I suppose, to bestow herself on his profligate brother.

ROWLEY. You know, Sir Peter, I have always taken the liberty to differ with you on the subject of these two young gentlemen. I only wish you may not be deceived in your opinion of the elder. For Charles, my life on't! he will retrieve his errors yet. Their worthy father, once my honoured master, was, at his years, nearly as wild a spark; yet, when he died, he did not leave a more benevolent heart to lament his loss.

SIR PETER. You are wrong, Master Rowley. On their father's death, you know, I acted as a kind of guardian to them both, till their uncle Sir Oliver's liberality gave them an early independence. Of course, no person could have more opportunities of judging of their hearts, and I was never mistaken in my life. Joseph is indeed a model for the young men of the age. He is a man of sentiment, and acts up to the sentiments he professes; but for the other, take my word for't, if he had any grain of virtue by descent, he has dissipated it with the rest of his inheritance. Ah! my old friend, Sir Oliver, will be deeply mortified when he finds how part of his bounty has been misapplied.

ROWLEY. I am sorry to find you so violent against the young man, because this may be the most critical period of his fortune. I came hither with news that will surprise you.

SIR PETER. What! let me hear.

ROWLEY. Sir Oliver is arrived, and at this moment in town.

SIR PETER. How! you astonish me! I thought you did not expect him this month.

ROWLEY. I did not: but his passage has been remarkably quick.

SIR PETER. Egad, I shall rejoice to see my old friend. 'Tis sixteen years since we met. We have had many a day together:—but does he still enjoin us not to inform his nephews of his arrival?

ROWLEY. Most strictly. He means, before it is known, to make some trial of their dispositions.

SIR PETER. Ah! there needs no art to discover their merits—however, he shall have his way, but, pray, does he know I am married?

ROWLEY. Yes, and will soon wish you joy.

SIR PETER. What, as we drink health to a friend in a consumption! Ah! Oliver will laugh at me. We used to rail at matrimony together, but he has been steady to his text. Well, he must be soon at my house, though—I'll instantly give orders for his reception. But, Master Rowley, don't drop a word that Lady Teazle and I ever disagree.

ROWLEY. By no means.

SIR PETER. For I should never be able to stand Noll's jokes; so I'll have him think, Lord forgive me! that we are a very happy couple.

ROWLEY. I understand you:—but then you must be very careful not to differ while he is in the house with you.

SIR PETER. Egad, and so we must—and that's impossible. Ah! Master Rowley, when an old bachelor marries a young wife, he deserves—no—the crime carries its punishment along with it. [Exeunt.]

· audience enjoy humour.
· going to persense in front of Sir P- they are perfect couple. Sir P would laugh if he knew they were teasing eachother.

## ACT II

### SCENE I

A Room in Sir PETER TEAZLE'S House [1]

[Enter SIR PETER and LADY TEAZLE.]

SIR PETER. Lady Teazle, Lady Teazle, I'll not bear it!

LADY TEAZLE. Sir Peter, Sir Peter you may bear it or not, as you please; but I ought to have my own way in everything, and, what's more, I will too. What! though I was educated in the country, I know very well that women of fashion in London are accountable to nobody after they are married.

SIR PETER. Very well, ma'am, very well; so a husband is to have no influence, no authority?

LADY TEAZLE. Authority! No, to be sure: if you wanted authority over me, you should have adopted me, and not married me: I'm sure you were old enough.

SIR PETER. Old enough!—ay, there it is. Well, well, Lady Teazle, though my life may be made unhappy by your temper, I'll not be ruined by your extravagance!

LADY TEAZLE. My extravagance! I'm sure I'm not more extravagant than a woman of fashion ought to be.

SIR PETER. No, no, madam, you shall throw away no more sums on such unmeaning luxury. 'Slife! to spend as much to furnish your dressing-room with flowers in winter as would suffice to turn the Pantheon into a greenhouse, and give a *fête champêtre* at Christmas.

LADY TEAZLE. And am I to blame, Sir Peter, because flowers are dear in cold weather? You should find fault with the climate, and not with me. For my part, I'm sure I wish it was spring all the year round, and that roses grew under our feet!

SIR PETER. Oons! madam—if you had been born to this, I shouldn't wonder at you talking thus; but you forget what your situation was when I married you.

LADY TEAZLE. No, no, I don't; 'twas a very disagreeable one, or I should never have married you.

SIR PETER. Yes, yes, madam, you were then in somewhat a humbler style—the daughter of a plain country squire. Recollect, Lady Teazle, when I saw you first sitting at your tambour, in a pretty figured linen gown, with a bunch of keys at your side, your hair combed smooth over a roll, and your apartment hung round with fruits in worsted, of your own working.

LADY TEAZLE. Oh, yes! I remember it very well, and a curious life I led. My daily occupation to inspect the dairy, superintend the poultry, make extracts from the family receipt-book, and comb my aunt Deborah's lapdog.

SIR PETER. Yes, yes, ma'am, 'twas so indeed.

LADY TEAZLE. And then you know, my evening amusements! To draw patterns for ruffles, which I had not materials to make up; to play Pope Joan with the curate; to read a sermon to my aunt; or to be stuck down to an old spinet to strum my father to sleep a after fox-chase.

SIR PETER. I am glad you have so good a memory. Yes, madam, these were the recreations I took you from! but now you must have your coach—*vis-à-vis*—and three powdered footmen before your chair; and, in the summer, a pair of white cats to draw you to Kensington Gardens. No recollection, I suppose, when you were content to ride double, behind the butler, on a docked coach-horse.

LADY TEAZLE. No—I swear I never did that: I deny the butler and the coach-horse.

SIR PETER. This, madam, was your situation; and what have I done for you? I have made you a woman of fashion, of fortune, of rank—in short, I have made you my wife.

LADY TEAZLE. Well, then, and there is but one thing more you can make me to add to the obligation, this is—

SIR PETER. My widow, I suppose?

LADY TEAZLE. Hem! hem!

SIR PETER. I thank you, madam—but don't flatter yourself, for, though your ill conduct may disturb my peace of mind, it shall never break my heart, I promise you: however, I am equally obliged to you for the hint.

LADY TEAZLE. Then why will you endeavour to make yourself so disagreeable to me, and thwart me in every little elegant expense?

SIR PETER. 'Slife, madam, I say, had you any of these little elegant expenses when you married me?

LADY TEAZLE. Lud, Sir Peter! would you have me be out of the fashion?

SIR PETER. The fashion, indeed! what had you to do with the fashion before you married me?

LADY TEAZLE. For my part, I should think you would like to have your wife thought a woman of taste.

SIR PETER. Ay—there again—taste! Zounds! madam, you had no taste when you married me!

LADY TEAZLE. That's very true, indeed, Sit Peter! and, after having married you, I should never pretend to taste again, I allow. But now, Sir Peter, since we have finished our daily jangle, I presume I may go to my engagement at Lady Sneerwell's.

SIR PETER. Ay, there's another precious circumstance—a charming set of acquaintance you have made there!

LADY TEAZLE. Nay, Sir Peter, they are all people of rank and fortune, and remarkably tenacious of reputation.

SIR PETER. Yes, egad, they are tenacious of reputation with a vengeance; for they don't choose anybody should have a character but themselves! Such a crew! Ah! many a wretch has rid on a hurdle who has done less mischief than these utterers of forged tales, coiners of scandal, and clippers of reputation.

LADY TEAZLE. What, would you restrain the freedom of speech?

SIR PETER. Ah! they have made you just as bad as any one of the society.

LADY TEAZLE. Why, I believe I do bear a part with a miserable grace.

SIR PETER. Grace indeed!

LADY TEAZLE. But I vow I bear no malice against the people I abuse: when I say an ill-natured thing, 'tis out of pure good humour; and I take it for granted they deal exactly in the same manner with me. But, Sir Peter, you know you promised to come to Lady Sneerwell's too.

SIR PETER. Well, well, I'll call in, just to look after my own character.

LADY TEAZLE. Then, indeed, you must make haste after me, or you'll be too late. So goodbye to ye. [Exit.]

SIR PETER. So—I have gained much by my intended expostulation! Yet with what a charming air she contradicts every thing I say, and how pleasantly she shows her contempt for my authority! Well, though I can't make her love me, there is great satisfaction in quarrelling with her; and I think she never appears to such advantage as when she is doing every thing in her power to plague me. [Exit.]

## SCENE II

A Room in LADY SNEERWELL'S House

[LADY SNEERWELL, MRS. CANDOUR, CRABTREE, SIR BENJAMIN BACKBITE, and JOSEPH SURFACE, discovered.]

LADY SNEERWELL. Nay, positively, we will hear it.
JOSEPH. Yes, yes, the epigram, by all means.
SIR BENJAMIN. O plague on't, uncle! 'tis mere nonsense.
CRABTREE. No, no; 'fore Gad, very clever for an extempore!
SIR BENJAMIN. But, ladies, you should be acquainted with the circumstance. You must know, that one day last week, as Lady Betty Curricle was taking the dust in Hyde Park, in a sort of duodecimo phaeton, she desired me to write some verses on her ponies; upon which, I took out my pocket-book, and in a moment produced the following:—

Sure never were seen two such beautiful ponies;
Other horses are clowns, but these macaronies:
To give them this title I'm sure can't be wrong,
Their legs are so slim, and their tails are so long.

CRABTREE. There, ladies, done in the smack of a whip, and on horseback too.
JOSEPH. A very Phoebus, mounted—indeed, Sir Benjamin!
SIR BENJAMIN. Oh dear, sir! trifles—trifles.

[Enter LADY TEAZLE and MARIA.]

MRS. CANDOUR. I must have a copy.
LADY SNEERWELL. Lady Teazle, I hope we shall see Sir Peter?
LADY TEAZLE. I believe he'll wait on your ladyship presently.
LADY SNEERWELL. Maria, my love, you look grave. Come, you shall sit down to piquet with Mr. Surface.
MARIA. I take very little pleasure in cards—however, I'll do as your ladyship pleases.
LADY TEAZLE. [Aside.] I am surprised Mr. Surface should sit down with her; I thought he would have embraced this opportunity of speaking to me before Sir Peter came.

MRS. CANDOUR. Now, I'll die, but you are so scandalous, I'll forswear your society.

LADY TEAZLE. What's the matter, Mrs. Candour?

MRS. CANDOUR. They'll not allow our friend Miss Vermilion to be handsome.

LADY SNEERWELL. Oh, surely she is a pretty woman.

CRABTREE. I am very glad you think so, ma'am.

MRS. CANDOUR. She has a charming fresh colour.

LADY TEAZLE. Yes, when it is fresh put on.

MRS. CANDOUR. Oh, fie! I'll swear her colour is natural: I have seen it come and go!

LADY TEAZLE. I dare swear you have, ma'am: it goes off at night, and comes again in the morning.

SIR BENJAMIN. True, ma'am, it not only comes and goes; but, what's more, egad, her maid can fetch and carry it!

MRS. CANDOUR. Ha! ha! ha! how I hate to hear you talk so! But surely, now, her sister is, or was, very handsome.

CRABTREE. Who? Mrs. Evergreen? O Lord! she's six-and-fifty if she's an hour!

MRS. CANDOUR. Now positively you wrong her; fifty-two or fifty-three is the utmost—and I don't think she looks more.

SIR BENJAMIN. Ah! there's no judging by her looks, unless one could see her face.

LADY SNEERWELL. Well, well, if Mrs. Evergreen does take some pains to repair the ravages of time, you must allow she effects it with great ingenuity; and surely that's better than the careless manner in which the widow Ochre caulks her wrinkles.

SIR BENJAMIN. Nay, now, Lady Sneerwell, you are severe upon the widow. Come, come, 'tis not that she paints so ill—but, when she has finished her face, she joins it on so badly to her neck, that she looks like a mended statute, in which the connoisseur may see at once that the head is modern, though the trunk's antique.

CRABTREE. Ha! ha! ha! Well said, nephew!

MRS. CANDOUR. Ha! ha! ha! Well, you make me laugh; but I vow I hate you for it. What do you think of Miss Simper?

SIR BENJAMIN. Why, she has very pretty teeth.

LADY TEAZLE. Yes; and on that account, when she is neither speaking nor laughing (which very seldom happens), she never absolutely shuts her mouth, but leaves it always a-jar, as it were—thus. [Shows her teeth.]

MRS. CANDOUR. How can you be so ill-natured?

LADY TEAZLE. Nay, I allow even that's better than the pains Mrs. Prim takes to conceal her losses in front. She draws her mouth till it positively resembles the aperture of a poor's-box, and all her words appear to slide out edgewise, as it were—thus: *How do you do, madam? Yes, madam*. [Mimics.]

LADY SNEERWELL. Very well, Lady Teazle; I see you can be a little severe.

LADY TEAZLE. In defence of a friend it is but justice. But here comes Sir Peter to spoil our pleasantry.

[Enter SIR PETER TEAZLE.]

SIR PETER. Ladies, your most obedient.—[Aside.] Mercy on me, here is the whole set! a character dead at every word, I suppose.

MRS. CANDOUR. I am rejoiced you are come, Sir Peter. They have been so censorious—and Lady Teazle as bad as any one.

SIR PETER. That must be very distressing to you, indeed, Mrs. Candour.

MRS. CANDOUR. Oh, they will allow good qualities to nobody; not even good nature to our friend Mrs. Pursy.

LADY TEAZLE. What, the fat dowager who was at Mrs. Quadrille's last night?

MRS. CANDOUR. Nay, her bulk is her misfortune; and when she takes so much pains to get rid of it, you ought not to reflect on her.

LADY SNEERWELL. That's very true, indeed.

LADY TEAZLE. Yes, I know she almost lives on acids and small whey; laces herself by pulleys; and often, in the hottest noon in summer, you may see her on a little squat pony, with her hair plaited up behind like a drummer's and puffing round the Ring on a full trot.

MRS. CANDOUR. I thank you, Lady Teazle, for defending her.

SIR PETER. Yes, a good defence, truly.

MRS. CANDOUR. Truly, Lady Teazle is as censorious as Miss Sallow.

CRABTREE. Yes, and she is a curious being to pretend to be censorious—an awkward gawky, without any one good point under heaven.

MRS. CANDOUR. Positively you shall not be so very severe. Miss Sallow is a near relation of mine by marriage, and, as for her person, great allowance is to be made; for, let me tell you, a woman labours under many disadvantages who tries to pass for a girl of six-and-thirty.

LADY SNEERWELL. Though, surely, she is handsome still—and for the weakness in her eyes, considering how much she reads by candlelight, it is not to be wondered at.

MRS. CANDOUR. True, and then as to her manner; upon my word I think it is particularly graceful, considering she never had the least education: for you know her mother was a Welsh milliner, and her father a sugar-baker at Bristol.

SIR BENJAMIN. Ah! you are both of you too good-natured!

SIR PETER. [Aside.] Yes, damned good-natured! This their own relation! mercy on me!

MRS. CANDOUR. For my part, I own I cannot bear to hear a friend ill spoken of.

SIR PETER. No, to be sure!

SIR BENJAMIN. Oh! you are of a moral turn. Mrs. Candour and I can sit for an hour and hear Lady Stucco talk sentiment.

LADY TEAZLE. Nay, I vow Lady Stucco is very well with the dessert after dinner; for she's just like the French fruit one cracks for mottoes—made up of paint and proverb.

MRS. CANDOUR. Well, I will never join in ridiculing a friend; and so I constantly tell my cousin Ogle, and you all know what pretensions she has to be critical on beauty.

CRABTREE. Oh, to be sure! she has herself the oddest countenance that ever was seen; 'tis a collection of features from all the different countries of the globe.

SIR BENJAMIN. So she has, indeed—an Irish front—

CRABTREE. Caledonian locks—

SIR BENJAMIN. Dutch nose—

CRABTREE. Austrian lips—

SIR BENJAMIN. Complexion of a Spaniard—

CRABTREE. And teeth à la Chinoise—

SIR BENJAMIN. In short, her face resembles a *table d'hôte* at Spa—where no two guests are of a nation—

CRABTREE. Or a congress at the close of a general war—wherein all the members, even to her eyes, appear to have a different interest, and her nose and chin are the only parties likely to join issue.

MRS. CANDOUR. Ha! ha! ha!

SIR PETER. [Aside.] Mercy on my life!—a person they dine with twice a week.

MRS. CANDOUR. Nay, but I vow you shall not carry the laugh off so—forgive me leave to say, that Mrs. Ogle—

SIR PETER. Madam, madam, I beg your pardon—there's no stopping these good gentlemen's tongues. But when I tell you, Mrs.

Candour, that the lady they are abusing is a particular friend of mine, I hope you'll not take her part.

LADY SNEERWELL. Ha! ha! ha! well said, Sir Peter! but you are a cruel creature—too phlegmatic yourself for a jest, and too peevish to allow wit in others.

SIR PETER. Ah, madam, true wit is more nearly allied to good nature than your ladyship is aware of.

LADY TEAZLE. True, Sir Peter: I believe they are so near akin that they can never be united.

SIR BENJAMIN. Or rather, suppose them man and wife, because one seldom sees them together.

LADY TEAZLE. But Sir Peter is such an enemy to scandal, I believe he would have it put down by parliament.

SIR PETER. 'Fore heaven, madam, if they were to consider the sporting with reputation of as much importance as poaching on manors, and pass an act for the preservation of fame, as well as game, I believe many would thank them for the bill.

LADY SNEERWELL. O Lud! Sir Peter; would you deprive us of our privileges?

SIR PETER. Ay, madam; and then no person should be permitted to kill characters and run down reputations, but qualified old maids and disappointed widows.

LADY SNEERWELL. Go, you monster!

MRS. CANDOUR. But surely, you would not be quite so severe on those who only report what they hear?

SIR PETER. Yes, madam, I would have law merchant for them too; and in all cases of slander currency, whenever the drawer of the lie was not to be found, the injured parties should have a right to come on any of the endorsers.

CRABTREE. Well, for my part, I believe there never was a scandalous tale without some foundation.

LADY SNEERWELL. Come, ladies, shall we sit down to cards in the next room?

[Enter SERVANT, who whispers SIR PETER.]

SIR PETER. I'll be with them directly.—[Exit SERVANT.] [Aside.] I'll get away unperceived.

LADY SNEERWELL. Sir Peter, you are not going to leave us?

SIR PETER. Your ladyship must excuse me; I'm called away by particular business. But I leave my character behind me. [Exit.]

SIR BENJAMIN. Well—certainly, Lady Teazle, that lord of yours is a strange being: I could tell you some stories of him would make you laugh heartily if he were not your husband.

LADY TEAZLE. Oh, pray don't mind that; come, do let's hear them. [Exeunt all but JOSEPH SURFACE and MARIA.]

JOSEPH. Maria, I see you have no satisfaction in this society.

MARIA. How is it possible I should? If to raise malicious smiles at the infirmities or misfortunes of those who have never injured us be the province of wit or humour, Heaven grant me a double portion of dullness!

JOSEPH. Yet they appear more ill-natured than they are; they have no malice at heart.

MARIA. Then is their conduct still more contemptible; for, in my opinion, nothing could excuse the intemperance of their tongues but a natural and uncontrollable bitterness of mind.

JOSEPH. Undoubtedly, madam; and it has always been a sentiment of mine, that to propagate a malicious truth wantonly is more despicable than to falsify from revenge. But can you, Maria, feel thus for others, and be unkind to me alone? Is hope to be denied the tenderest passion?

MARIA. Why will you distress me by renewing this subject?

JOSEPH. Ah, Maria! you would not treat me thus, and oppose your guardian, Sir Peter's will, but that I see that profligate Charles is still a favoured rival.

MARIA. Ungenerously urged! But, whatever my sentiments are for that unfortunate young man, be assured I shall not feel more bound to give him up, because his distresses have lost him the regard even of a brother.

JOSEPH. Nay, but, Maria, do not leave me with a frown: by all that is honest, I swear— [Kneels.]

[Re-enter LADY TEAZLE behind.]

[Aside.] Gad's life, here's Lady Teazle.—[Aloud to MARIA.] You must not—no, you shall not—for, though I have the greatest regard for Lady Teazle—

MARIA. Lady Teazle!

JOSEPH. Yet were Sir Peter to suspect—

LADY TEAZLE. [Coming forward.] What is this, pray? Does he take her for me?—Child, you are wanted in the next room.—[Exit MARIA.] What is all this, pray?

JOSEPH. Oh, the most unlucky circumstance in nature! Maria has somehow suspected the tender concern I have for your happiness, and threatened to acquaint Sir Peter with her suspicions, and I was just endeavouring to reason with her when you came in.

LADY TEAZLE. Indeed! but you seemed to adopt a very tender mode of reasoning—do you usually argue on your knees?

JOSEPH. Oh, she's a child, and I thought a little bombast—But, Lady Teazle, when are you to give me your judgment on my library, as you promised?

LADY TEAZLE. No, no; I begin to think it would be imprudent, and you know I admit you as a lover no farther than fashion requires.

JOSEPH. True—a mere Platonic cicisbeo, what every wife is entitled to.

LADY TEAZLE. Certainly, one must not be out of the fashion. However, I have so many of my country prejudices left, that, though Sir Peter's ill humour may vex me ever so, it never shall provoke me to—

JOSEPH. The only revenge in your power. Well, I applaud your moderation.

LADY TEAZLE. Go—you are an insinuating wretch! But we shall be missed— let us join the company.

JOSEPH. But we had best not return together.

LADY TEAZLE. Well, don't stay; for Maria shan't come to hear any more of your reasoning, I promise you. [Exit.]

JOSEPH. A curious dilemma, truly, my politics have run me into! I wanted, at first, only to ingratiate myself with Lady Teazle, that she might not be my enemy with Maria; and I have, I don't know how, become her serious lover. Sincerely I begin to wish I had never made such a point of gaining so very good a character, for it has led me into so many cursed rogueries that I doubt I shall be exposed at last. [Exit.]

## SCENE III

A Room in SIR PETER TEAZLE'S House

[Enter SIR OLIVER SURFACE and ROWLEY.]

SIR OLIVER. Ha! ha! ha! so my old friend is married, hey?—a young wife out of the country. Ha! ha! ha! that he should have stood bluff to old bachelor so long, and sink into a husband at last!

ROWLEY. But you must not rally him on the subject, Sir Oliver; 'tis a tender point, I assure you, though he has been married only seven months.

SIR OLIVER. Then he has been just half a year on the stool of repentance!—Poor Peter! But you say he has entirely given up Charles—never sees him, hey?

ROWLEY. His prejudice against him is astonishing, and I am sure greatly increased by a jealousy of him with Lady Teazle, which he has industriously been led into by a scandalous society in the neighbourhood, who have contributed not a little to Charles' ill name. Whereas the truth is, I believe, if the lady is partial to either of them, his brother is the favourite.

SIR OLIVER. Ay, I know there are a set of malicious, prating, prudent gossips, both male and female, who murder characters to kill time, and will rob a young fellow of his good name before he has years to know the value of it. But I am not to be prejudiced against my nephew by such, I promise you! No, no: if Charles has done nothing false or mean, I shall compound for his extravagance.

ROWLEY. Then, my life on't, you will reclaim him. Ah, sir, it gives me new life to find that your heart is not turned against him, and that the son of my good old master has one friend, however, left.

SIR OLIVER. What! shall I forget, Master Rowley, when I was at his years myself? Egad, my brother and I were neither of us very prudent youths; and yet, I believe, you have not seen many better men than your old master was?

ROWLEY. Sir, 'tis this reflection gives me assurance that Charles may yet be a credit to his family. But here comes Sir Peter.

SIR OLIVER. Egad, so he does! Mercy on me! he's greatly altered, and seems to have a settled married look! One may read husband in his face at this distance!

[Enter SIR PETER TEAZLE.]

SIR PETER. Ha! Sir Oliver—my old friend! Welcome to England a thousand times!

SIR OLIVER. Thank you, thank you, Sir Peter! and i'faith I am glad to find you well, believe me!

SIR PETER. Oh! 'tis a long time since we met—fifteen years, I doubt, Sir Oliver, and many a cross accident in the time.

SIR OLIVER. Ay, I have had my share. But what! I find you are married, hey, my old boy? Well, well, it can't be helped; and so—I wish you joy with all my heart!

SIR PETER. Thank you, thank you, Sir Oliver.—Yes, I have entered into— the happy state; but we'll not talk of that now.

SIR OLIVER. True, true, Sir Peter; old friends should not begin on grievances at first meeting. No, no, no.

ROWLEY. [Aside to SIR OLIVER.] Take care, pray, sir.

SIR OLIVER. Well, so one of my nephews is a wild rogue, hey?

SIR PETER. Wild! Ah! my old friend, I grieve for your disappointment there; he's a lost young man, indeed. However, his brother will make you amends; Joseph is, indeed, what a youth should be—every body in the world speaks well of him.

SIR OLIVER. I am sorry to hear it; he has too good a character to be an honest fellow. Every body speaks well of him! Pshaw! then he has bowed as low to knaves and fools as to the honest dignity of genius and virtue.

SIR PETER. What, Sir Oliver! do you blame him for not making enemies?

SIR OLIVER. Yes, if he has merit enough to deserve them.

SIR PETER. Well, well—you'll be convinced when you know him. 'Tis edification to bear him converse; he professes the noblest sentiments.

SIR OLIVER. Oh, plague of his sentiments! If he salutes me with a scrap of morality in his mouth, I shall be sick directly. But, however, don't mistake me, Sir Peter; I don't mean to defend Charles' errors: but, before I form my judgment of either of them, I intend to make a trial of their hearts; and my friend Rowley and I have planned something for the purpose.

ROWLEY. And Sir Peter shall own for once he has been mistaken.

SIR PETER. Oh, my life on Joseph's honour!

SIR OLIVER. Well—come, give us a bottle of good wine, and we'll drink the lads' health, and tell you our scheme.

SIR PETER. *Allons*, then!

comparision
himself
Joseph as a young man.
his belief of youth.



not angels

SIR OLIVER. And don't, Sir Peter, be so severe against your old friend's son. Odds my life! I am not sorry that he has run out of the course a little: for my part, I hate to see prudence clinging to the green suckers of youth; 'tis like ivy round a sapling, and spoils the growth of the tree. [Exeunt.]

prudence clinging to youth.
seeming too good

Sir Olive knows more of Joseph
if everyone thinks that, he is
at the level of the gossips
scandals

Joseph a man of sentiments

- he will spy on them, to test which one is true
- moral man? sentiments? I'll be sick
- trial of their hearts - test them - make their judgement
- emotive language

## ACT III

### SCENE I

A Room in SIR PETER TEAZLE'S House

[Enter SIR PETER TEAZLE,
SIR OLIVER SURFACE, and ROWLEY.]

SIR PETER. Well, then, we will see this fellow first, and have our wine afterwards. But how is this, Master Rowley? I don't see the jest of your scheme.

ROWLEY. Why, sir, this Mr. Stanley, whom I was speaking of, is nearly related to them by their mother. He was once a merchant in Dublin, but has been ruined by a series of undeserved misfortunes. He has applied, by letter, since his confinement, both to Mr. Surface and Charles: from the former he has received nothing but evasive promises of future service, while Charles has done all that his extravagance has left him power to do; and he is, at this time, endeavouring to raise a sum of money, part of which, in the midst of his own distresses, I know he intends for the service of poor Stanley.

SIR OLIVER. Ah! he is my brother's son.

SIR PETER. Well, but how is Sir Oliver personally to—

ROWLEY. Why, sir, I will inform Charles and his brother that Stanley has obtained permission to apply personally to his friends; and, as they have neither of them ever seen him, let Sir Oliver assume his character, and he will have a fair opportunity of judging, at least, of the benevolence of their dispositions: and believe me, sir, you will find in the youngest brother one who, in the midst of folly and dissipation, has still, as our immortal bard expresses it,—

"a heart to pity, and a hand,
Open as day, for meeting charity."

SIR PETER. Pshaw! What signifies his having an open hand or purse either, when he has nothing left to give? Well, well, make the trial, if you please. But where is the fellow whom you brought for Sir Oliver to examine, relative to Charles' affairs?

ROWLEY. Below, waiting his commands, and no one can give him better intelligence.—This, Sir Oliver, is a friendly Jew, who, to do him justice, had done every thing in his power to bring your nephew to a proper sense of his extravagance.

SIR PETER. Pray let us have him in.

ROWLEY. Desire Mr. Moses to walk up stairs. [Calls to SERVANT.]

SIR PETER. But, pray, why should you suppose he will speak the truth?

ROWLEY. Oh, I have, convinced him that he has no chance of recovering certain sums advanced to Charles but through the bounty of Sir Oliver, who he knows is arrived; so that your may depend on his fidelity to his own interests. I have another evidence in my power, one Snake, whom I have detected in a matter little short of forgery, and shall shortly produce to remove some of your prejudices, Sir Peter, relative to Charles and Lady Teazle.

SIR PETER. I have heard too much on that subject.

ROWLEY. Here comes the honest Israelite.

[Enter MOSES.]

—This is Sir Oliver.

SIR OLIVER. Sir, I understand you have lately had great dealings with my nephew Charles?

MOSES. Yes, Sir Oliver, I have done all I could for him; but he was ruined before he came to me for assistance.

SIR OLIVER. That was unlucky, truly; for you have had no opportunity of showing your talents.

MOSES. None at all; I hadn't the pleasure of knowing his distresses till he was some thousands worse than nothing.

SIR OLIVER. Unfortunate, indeed! But I suppose you have done all in your power for him, honest Moses?

MOSES. Yes, he knows that. This very evening I was to have brought him a gentleman from the city, who does not know him, and will, I believe, advance him some money.

SIR PETER. What, one Charles has never had money from before?

MOSES. Yes, Mr. Premium, of Crutched Friars, formerly a broker.

SIR PETER. Egad, Sir Oliver, a thought strikes me!—Charles, you say, does not know Mr. Premium?

MOSES. Not at all.

SIR PETER. Now then, Sir Oliver, you may have a better opportunity of satisfying yourself than by an old romancing tale of a poor relation: go with my friend Moses, and represent Premium, and then, I'll answer for it, you'll see your nephew in all his glory.

SIR OLIVER. Egad, I like this idea better than the other, and I may visit Joseph afterwards as old Stanley.

SIR PETER. True—so you may.

ROWLEY. Well, this is taking Charles rather at a disadvantage, to be sure. However, Moses, you understand Sir Peter, and will be faithful?

MOSES. You may depend upon me.—[Looks at his watch.] This is near the time I was to have gone.

SIR OLIVER. I'll accompany you as soon as you please, Moses—But hold! I have forgot one thing—how the plague shall I be able to pass for a Jew?

MOSES. There's no need—the principal is Christian.

SIR OLIVER. Is he? I'm very sorry to hear it. But, then again, ain't I rather too smartly dressed to look like a money lender?

SIR PETER. Not at all; 'twould not be out of character, if you went in your own carriage—would it, Moses?

MOSES. Not in the least.

SIR OLIVER. Well, but how must I talk; there's certainly some cant of usury and mode of treating that I ought to know?

SIR PETER. Oh, there's not much to learn. The great point, as I take it, is to be exorbitant enough in your demands. Hey, Moses?

MOSES. Yes, that's a very great point.

SIR OLIVER. I'll answer for't I'll not be wanting in that. I'll ask him eight or ten per cent. on the loan, at least.

MOSES. If you ask him no more than that, you'll be discovered immediately.

SIR OLIVER. Hey! what, the plague! how much then?

MOSES. That depends upon the circumstances. If he appears not very anxious for the supply, you should require only forty or fifty per cent.; but if you find him in great distress, and want the moneys very bad, you may ask double.

SIR PETER. A good honest trade you're learning, Sir Oliver!

SIR OLIVER. Truly, I think so—and not unprofitable.

MOSES. Then, you know, you haven't the moneys yourself, but are forced to borrow them for him of a friend.

SIR OLIVER. Oh! I borrow it of a friend, do I?

MOSES. And your friend is an unconscionable dog: but you can't help that.

SIR OLIVER. My friend an unconscionable dog, is he?

MOSES. Yes, and he himself has not the moneys by him, but is forced to sell stock at a great loss.

SIR OLIVER. He is forced to sell stock at a great loss, is he? Well, that's very kind of him.

SIR PETER. I' faith, Sir Oliver—Mr. Premium, I mean—you'll soon be master of the trade. But, Moses! would not you have him run out a little against the Annuity Bill? That would be in character, I should think.

MOSES. Very much.

ROWLEY. And lament that a young man now must be at years of discretion before he is suffered to ruin himself?

MOSES. Ay, great pity!

SIR PETER. And abuse the public for allowing merit to an act whose only object is to snatch misfortune and imprudence from the rapacious gripe of usury, and give the minor a chance of inheriting his estate without being undone by coming into possession.

SIR OLIVER. So, so—Moses shall give me farther instructions as we go together.

SIR PETER. You will not have much time, for your nephew lives hard by.

SIR OLIVER. Oh, never fear! my tutor appears so able, that though Charles lived in the next street, it must be my own fault if I am not a complete rogue before I turn the corner. [Exit with MOSES.]

SIR PETER. So, now, I think Sir Oliver will be convinced: you are partial, Rowley, and would have prepared Charles for the other plot.

ROWLEY. No, upon my word, Sir Peter.

SIR PETER. Well, go bring me this Snake, and I'll hear what he has to say presently. I see Maria, and want to speak with her.—[Exit ROWLEY.] I should be glad to be convinced my suspicions of Lady Teazle and Charles were unjust. I have never yet opened my mind on this subject to my friend Joseph—I am determined I will do it—he will give me his opinion sincerely.

[Enter MARIA.]

So, child, has Mr. Surface returned with you?

MARIA. No, sir; he was engaged.

SIR PETER. Well, Maria, do you not reflect, the more you converse with that amiable young man, what return his partiality for you deserves?

MARIA. Indeed, Sir Peter, your frequent importunity on this subject distresses me extremely—you compel me to declare, that I know no man who has ever paid me a particular attention whom I would not prefer to Mr. Surface.

SIR PETER. So—here's perverseness! No, no, Maria, 'tis Charles only whom you would prefer. 'Tis evident his vices and follies have won your heart.

MARIA. This is unkind, sir. You know I have obeyed you in neither seeing nor corresponding with him: I have heard enough to convince me that he is unworthy my regard. Yet I cannot think it culpable, if while my understanding severely condemns his vices, my heart suggests some pity for his distresses.

SIR PETER. Well, well, pity him as much as you please; but give your heart and hand to a worthier object.

MARIA. Never to his brother!

SIR PETER. Go, perverse and obstinate! But take care, madam; you have never yet known what the authority of a guardian is: don't compel me to inform you of it.

MARIA. I can only say, you shall not have just reason. 'Tis true, by my father's will, I am for a short period bound to regard you as his substitute; but must cease to think you so, when you would compel me to be miserable. [Exit.]

SIR PETER. Was ever man so crossed as I am, every thing conspiring to fret me! I had not been involved in matrimony a fortnight, before her father, a hale and hearty man, died, on purpose, I believe, for the pleasure of plaguing me with the care of his daughter.—[LADY TEAZLE sings without.] But here comes my helpmate! She appears in great good humour. How happy I should be if I could tease her into loving me, though but a little!

[Enter LADY TEAZLE.]

LADY TEAZLE. Lud! Sir Peter, I hope you haven't been quarrelling with Maria? It is not using me well to be ill-humoured when I am not by.

SIR PETER. Ah, Lady Teazle, you might have the power to make me good humoured at all times.

LADY TEAZLE. I am sure I wish I had; for I want you to be in a charming sweet temper at this moment. Do be good humoured now, and let me have two hundred pounds, will you?

SIR PETER. Two hundred pounds; what, ain't I to be in a good humour without paying for it! But speak to me thus, and i' faith there's nothing I could refuse you. You shall have it; but seal me a bond for the repayment.

LADY TEAZLE. Oh, no—there—my note of hand will do as well. [Offering her hand.]

SIR PETER. And you shall no longer reproach me with not giving you an independent settlement. I mean shortly to surprise you: but shall we always live thus, hey?

LADY TEAZLE. If you please. I'm sure I don't care how soon we leave off quarrelling, provided you'll own you were tired first.

SIR PETER. Well—then let our future contest be, who shall be most obliging.

LADY TEAZLE. I assure you, Sir Peter, good nature becomes you. You look now as you did before we were married, when you used to walk with me under the elms, and tell me stories of what a gallant you were in your youth, and chuck me under the chin, you would; and asked me if I thought I could love an old fellow, who would deny me nothing—didn't you?

SIR PETER. Yes, yes, and you were as kind and attentive—

LADY TEAZLE. Ay, so I was, and would always take your part, when my acquaintance used to abuse you, and turn you into ridicule.

SIR PETER. Indeed!

LADY TEAZLE. Ay, and when my cousin Sophy has called you a stiff, peevish old bachelor, and laughed at me for thinking of marrying one who might be my father, I have always defended you, and said, I didn't think you so ugly by any means.

SIR PETER. Thank you.

LADY TEAZLE. And I dared say you'd make a very good sort of a husband.

SIR PETER. And you prophesied right; and we shall now be the happiest couple—

LADY TEAZLE. And never differ again?

SIR PETER. No, never!—though at the same time, indeed, my dear Lady Teazle, you must watch your temper very seriously; for in all our little quarrels, my dear, if you recollect, my love, you always began first.

LADY TEAZLE. I beg your pardon, my dear Sir Peter: indeed, you always gave the provocation.

SIR PETER. Now see, my angel! take care—contradicting isn't the way to keep friends.

LADY TEAZLE. Then don't you begin it, my love!

SIR PETER. There, now! you—you are going on. You don't perceive, my life, that you are just doing the very thing which you know always makes me angry.

LADY TEAZLE. Nay, you know, if you will be angry without any reason, my dear—

SIR PETER. There! now you want to quarrel again.

LADY TEAZLE. No, I'm sure I don't: but, if you will be so peevish—

SIR PETER. There now! who begins first?

LADY TEAZLE. Why, you, to be sure. I said nothing—but there's no bearing your temper.

SIR PETER. No, no, madam: the fault's in your own temper.

LADY TEAZLE. Ay, you are just what my cousin Sophy said you would be.

SIR PETER. Your cousin Sophy is a forward, impertinent gipsy.

LADY TEAZLE. You are a great bear, I'm sure, to abuse my relations.

SIR PETER. Now may all the plagues of marriage be doubled on me, if ever I try to be friends with you any more!

LADY TEAZLE. So much the better.

SIR PETER. No, no, madam: 'tis evident you never cared a pin for me, and I was a madman to marry you—a pert, rural coquette, that had refused half the honest squires in the neighbourhood!

LADY TEAZLE. And I am sure I was a fool to marry you—an old dangling bachelor, who was single at fifty, only because he never could meet with any one who would have him.

SIR PETER. Ay, ay, madam; but you were pleased enough to listen to me: you never had such an offer before.

LADY TEAZLE. No! didn't I refuse Sir Tivy Terrier, who every body said would have been a better match? for his estate is just as good as yours, and he has broke his neck since we have been married.

SIR PETER. I have done with you, madam! You are an unfeeling, ungrateful—but there's an end of everything. I believe you capable of everything that is bad. Yes, madam, I now believe the reports relative to you and Charles, madam. Yes, madam, you and Charles are, not without grounds—

LADY TEAZLE. Take care, Sir Peter! you had better not insinuate any such thing! I'll not be suspected without cause, I promise you.

SIR PETER. Very well, madam! very well! A separate maintenance as soon as please. Yes, madam or a divorce! I'll make an example of myself for the benefit of all old bachelors. Let us separate, madam.

LADY TEAZLE. Agreed! agreed! And now, my dear Sir Peter, we are of a mind once more, we may be the happiest couple, and never differ again, you know: ha! ha! ha! Well, you are going to be in a passion, I see, and I shall only interrupt you—so, bye! bye! [Exit.]

SIR PETER. Plagues and tortures! can't I make her angry either! Oh, I am the most miserable fellow! But I'll not bear her presuming to keep her temper: no! she may break my heart, but she shan't keep her temper. [Exit.]

joke about divorce
Sir Peter cant make her angry.

## SCENE II

A Room in CHARLES SURFACE'S House

[Enter TRIP, MOSES, and SIR OLIVER SURFACE.]

TRIP. Here, Master Moses! if you'll stay a moment I'll try whether—what's the gentleman's name?

SIR OLIVER. [Aside to MOSES.] Mr. Moses, what is my name?

MOSES. Mr. Premium.

TRIP. Premium—very well. [Exit taking snuff.]

SIR OLIVER. To judge by the servants, one wouldn't believe the master was ruined. But what!—sure, this was my brother's house?

MOSES. Yes, sir; Mr. Charles bought it of Mr. Joseph, with the furniture, pictures, &c., just as the old gentleman left it. Sir Peter thought it a piece of extravagance in him.

SIR OLIVER. In my mind, the other's economy in selling it to him was more reprehensible by half.

[Re-enter TRIP.]

TRIP. My master says you must wait, gentlemen: he has company, and can't speak with you yet.

SIR OLIVER. If he knew who it was wanted to see him, perhaps he would not send such a message.

TRIP. Yes, yes, sir; he knows you are here—I did not forget little Premium: no, no, no.

SIR OLIVER. Very well; and I pray, sir, what may be your name?

TRIP. Trip, sir; my name is Trip, at your service.

SIR OLIVER. Well, then, Mr. Trip, you have a pleasant sort of place here, I guess?

TRIP. Why, yes—here are three or four of us pass our time agreeably enough; but then our wages are sometimes a little in arrear—and not very great either—but fifty pounds a year, and find our own bags and bouquets.

SIR OLIVER. [Aside.] Bags and bouquets! halters and bastinadoes!

TRIP. And *à propos*, Moses, have you been able to get me that little bill discounted?

SIR OLIVER. [Aside.] Wants to raise money too!—mercy on me! Has his distresses too, I warrant, like a lord, and affects creditors and duns.

MOSES. 'Twas not to be done, indeed, Mr. Trip.

TRIP. Good luck, you surprise me! My friend Brush has indorsed it, and I thought when he put his name at the back of a bill 'twas the same as cash.

MOSES. No, 'twouldn't do.

TRIP. A small sum—but twenty pounds. Hark'ee, Moses, do you think you couldn't get it me by way of annuity?

SIR OLIVER. [Aside.] An annuity! ha! ha! a footman raise money by way of annuity. Well done, luxury, egad!

MOSES. Well, but you must insure your place.

TRIP. Oh, with all my heart! I'll insure my place, and my life too, if you please.

SIR OLIVER. [Aside.] It's more than I would your neck.

MOSES. But is there nothing you could deposit?

TRIP. Why, nothing capital of my master's wardrobe has dropped lately; but I could give you a mortgage on some of his winter clothes, with equity of redemption before November—or you shall have the reversion of the French velvet, or a post-obit on the blue and silver;—these, I should think, Moses, with a few pair of point ruffles, as a collateral security—hey, my little fellow?

MOSES. Well, well. [Bell rings.]

TRIP. Egad, I heard the bell. I believe, gentlemen, I can now introduce you. Don't forget the annuity, little Moses! This way, gentlemen, I'll insure my place, you know.

trip reflection on charles

SIR OLIVER. [Aside.] If the man be a shadow of the master, this is the temple of dissipation indeed! [Exeunt.]

things are worse than he thought indeed

important

Charles has no money
trip-servant- his lifestyle
Sir Oliver is gassed at this.

## SCENE III

Another Room in the same

[CHARLES SURFACE, SIR HARRY BUMPER, CARELESS, and Gentlemen, discovered drinking.]

CHARLES. 'Fore heaven, 'tis true!—there's the great degeneracy of the age. Many of our acquaintance have taste, spirit, and politeness; but, plaque on 't, they won't drink.

CARELESS. It is so, indeed, Charles! they give into all the substantial luxuries of the table, and abstain from nothing but wine and wit. Oh, certainly society suffers by it intolerably! for now, instead of the social spirit of raillery that used to mantle over a glass of bright Burgundy, their conversation is become just like the Spa-water they drink, which has all the pertness and flatulency of champagne, without its spirit or flavour.

FIRST GENTLEMAN. But what are they to do who love play better than wine?

CARELESS. True! there's Sir Harry diets himself for gaming, and is now under a hazard regimen.

CHARLES. Then he'll have the worst of it. What! you wouldn't train a horse for the course by keeping him from corn? For my part, egad, I am never so successful as when I am a little merry: let me throw on a bottle of champagne, and I never lose.

ALL. Hey, what?

CARELESS. At least I never feel my losses, which is exactly the same thing.

SECOND GENTLEMAN. Ay, that I believe.

CHARLES. And then, what man can pretend to be a believer in love, who is an abjurer of wine? 'Tis the test by which the lover knows his own heart. Fill a dozen bumpers to a dozen beauties, and she that floats at the top is the maid that has bewitched you.

CARELESS. Now then, Charles, be honest, and give us your real favourite.

CHARLES. Why, I have withheld her only in compassion to you. If I toast her, you must give a round of her peers, which is impossible—on earth.

CARELESS. Oh! then we'll find some canonized vestals or heathen goddesses that will do, I warrant.

CHARLES. Here, then, bumpers, you rogues! bumpers! Maria! Maria!—

SIR HARRY. Maria who?

CHARLES. Oh, damn the surname!—'tis too formal to be registered in Love's calendar—Maria!

ALL. Maria! - merry, they all toast Maria

CHARLES. But now, Sir Harry, beware, we must have beauty superlative.

CARELESS. Nay, never study, Sir Harry: we'll stand to the toast, though your mistress should want an eye, and you know you have a song will excuse you.

SIR HARRY. Egad, so I have! and I'll give him the song instead of the lady. - more + more merry

[Sings.]

Here's to the maiden of bashful fifteen;
Here's to the widow of fifty;
Here's to the flaunting extravagant quean,
And here's to the housewife that's thrifty.

CHORUS. Let the toast pass,—
Drink to the lass,
I'll warrant she'll prove an excuse for the glass.

Here's to the charmer whose dimples we prize;
Now to the maid who has none, sir:
Here's to the girl with a pair of blue eyes,
And here's to the nymph with but one, sir.
CHORUS. Let the toast pass, &c.

Here's to the maid with a bosom of snow:
Now to her that's as brown as a berry:
Here's to the wife with a face full of woe,
And now to the damsel that's merry.
CHORUS. Let the toast pass, &c.

For let 'em be clumsy, or let 'em be slim,
Young or ancient, I care not a feather;
So fill a pint bumper quite up to the brim,
So fill up your glasses, nay, fill to the brim,
And let us e'en toast them together.
CHORUS. Let the toast pass, &c.

ALL. Bravo! bravo!

[Enter TRIP, and whispers CHARLES SURFACE.]

CHARLES. Gentlemen, you must excuse me a little.—Careless, take the chair, will you?

CARELESS. Nay, pr'ythee, Charles, what now? This is one of your peerless beauties, I suppose, has dropped in by chance?

CHARLES. No, faith! To tell you the truth, 'tis a Jew and a broker, who are come by appointment.

CARELESS. Oh, damn it! let's have the Jew in.

FIRST GENTLEMAN. Ay, and the broker too, by all means.

SECOND GENTLEMAN. Yes, yes, the Jew and the broker.

CHARLES. Egad, with all my heart!—Trip, bid the gentlemen walk in—[Exit TRIP.] Though there's one of them a stranger, I can tell you.

CARELESS. Charles, let us give them some generous Burgundy, and perhaps they'll grow conscientious.

CHARLES. Oh, hang 'em, no! wine does but draw forth a man's natural qualities; and to make them drink would only be to whet their knavery.

[Re-enter TRIP, with SIR OLIVER SURFACE and MOSES.]

CHARLES. So, honest Moses; walk in, pray, Mr. Premium—that's the gentleman's name, isn't it, Moses?

MOSES. Yes, sir.

CHARLES. Set chairs, Trip.—Sit down, Mr. Premium.—Glasses, Trip.—[TRIP gives chairs and glasses, and exit.] Sit down, Moses.—Come, Mr. Premium, I'll give you a sentiment; here's *Success to usury!*—Moses, fill the gentleman a bumper.

MOSES. Success to usury! [Drinks.]

CARELESS. Right, Moses—usury is prudence and industry, and deserves to succeed.

SIR OLIVER. Then here's—*All the success it deserves!* [Drinks.]

CARELESS. No, no, that won't do! Mr. Premium, you have demurred at the toast, and must drink it in a pint bumper.

FIRST GENTLEMAN. A pint bumper, at least.

MOSES. Oh, pray, sir, consider—Mr. Premium's a gentleman.

CARELESS. And therefore loves good wine.

SECOND GENTLEMAN. Give Moses a quart glass—this is mutiny, and a high contempt for the chair.

CARELESS. Here, now for 't! I'll see justice done to the last drop of my bottle.

SIR OLIVER. Nay, pray, gentlemen—I did not expect this usage.

CHARLES. No, hang it, you shan't; Mr. Premium's a stranger.

SIR OLIVER. [Aside.] Odd! I wish I was well out of their company.

CARELESS. Plague on 'em then! if they won't drink, we'll not sit down with them. Come, Harry, the dice are in the next room.—Charles, you'll join us when you have finished your business with the gentlemen?

CHARLES. I will! I will!—[Exeunt SIR HARRY BUMPER and GENTLEMEN; CARELESS following.] Careless!

CARELESS. [Returning.] Well!

CHARLES. Perhaps I may want you.

CARELESS. Oh, you know I am always ready: word, note, or bond, 'tis all the same to me. [Exit.]

MOSES. Sir, this is Mr. Premium, a gentleman of the strictest honour and secrecy; and always performs what he undertakes. Mr. Premium, this is—

CHARLES. Pshaw! have done. Sir, my friend Moses is a very honest fellow, but a little slow at expression: he'll be an hour giving us our titles. Mr. Premium, the plain state of the matter is this: I am an extravagant young fellow who wants to borrow money; you I take to be a prudent old fellow, who have got money to lend. I am block-head enough to give fifty per cent, sooner than not have it; and you, I presume, are rogue enough to take a hundred if you can get it. Now, sir, you see we are acquainted at once, and may proceed to business without further ceremony.

SIR OLIVER. Exceeding frank, upon my word. I see, sir, you are not a man of many compliments.

CHARLES. Oh, no sir! plain dealing in business I always think best.

SIR OLIVER. Sir, I like you better for it. However, you are mistaken in one thing; I have no money to lend, but I believe I could procure some of a friend; but then he's an unconscionable dog. Isn't he, Moses? And must sell stock to accommodate you. Mustn't he, Moses?

MOSES. Yes, indeed! You know I always speak the truth, and scorn to tell a lie!

CHARLES. Right. People that speak truth generally do. But these are trifles, Mr. Premium. What! I know money isn't to be bought without paying for't!

SIR OLIVER. Well, but what security could you give! You have no land, I suppose?

CHARLES. Not a mole-hill, nor a twig, but what's in the bough-pots out of the window!

SIR OLIVER. Nor any stock, I presume?

CHARLES. Nothing but live stock—and that's only a few pointers and ponies. But pray, Mr. Premium, are you acquainted at all with any of my connections?

SIR OLIVER. Why, to say truth, I am.

CHARLES. Then you must know that I have a devilish rich uncle in the East Indies, Sir Oliver Surface, from whom I have the greatest expectations?

SIR OLIVER. That you have a wealthy uncle, I have heard; but how your expectations will turn out is more, I believe, than you can tell.

CHARLES. Oh, no!—there can be no doubt. They tell me I'm a prodigious favourite, and that he talks of leaving me every thing.

SIR OLIVER. Indeed! this is the first I've heard of it.

CHARLES. Yes, yes, 'tis just so. Moses knows 'tis true; don't you, Moses?

MOSES. Oh, yes! I'll swear to't.

SIR OLIVER. [Aside.] Egad, they'll persuade me presently I'm at Bengal.

CHARLES. Now I propose, Mr. Premium, if it's agreeable to you, a post-obit on Sir Oliver's life: though at the same time the old fellow has been so liberal to me, that I give you my word, I should be very sorry to hear that any thing had happened to him.

SIR OLIVER. Not more than *I* should, I assure you. But the bond you mention happens to be just the worst security you could offer me—for I might live to a hundred and never see the principal.

CHARLES. Oh, yes, you would! the moment Sir Oliver dies, you know, you would come on me for the money.

SIR OLIVER. Then I believe I should be the most unwelcome dun you ever had in your life.

CHARLES. What! I suppose you're afraid that Sir Oliver is too good a life?

SIR OLIVER. No, indeed I am not; though I have heard he is as hale and healthy as any man of his years in Christendom.

CHARLES. There again, now, you are misinformed. No, no, the climate has hurt him considerably, poor uncle Oliver. Yes, yes, he breaks apace, I'm told—and is so much altered lately that his nearest relations would not know him.

SIR OLIVER. No! Ha! ha! ha! so much altered lately that his nearest relations would not know him! Ha! ha! ha! egad—ha! ha! ha!

CHARLES. Ha! ha!—you're glad to hear that, little Premium?

SIR OLIVER. No, no, I'm not.

CHARLES. Yes, yes, your are—ha! ha! ha!—you know that mends our chance.

SIR OLIVER. But I'm told Sir Oliver is coming over; nay, some say he is actually arrived.

CHARLES. Pshaw! sure I must know better than you whether he's come or not. No, no, rely on't he's at this moment at Calcutta. Isn't he, Moses?

MOSES. Oh, yes, certainly.

SIR OLIVER. Very true, as you say, you must know better than I, though I have it from pretty good authority. Haven't I, Moses?

MOSES. Yes, most undoubted!

SIR OLIVER. But, sir, as I understand you want a few hundreds immediately, is there nothing you could dispose of?

CHARLES. How do you mean?

SIR OLIVER. For instance, now, I have heard that your father left behind him a great quantity of massy old plate.

CHARLES. O Lud! that's gone long ago. Moses can tell you how better than I can.

SIR OLIVER. [Aside.] Good lack! all the family race-cups and corporation-bowls!—[Aloud.] Then it was also supposed that his library was one of the most valuable and compact.

CHARLES. Yes, yes, so it was—vastly too much so for a private gentleman. For any part, I was always of a communicative disposition, so I thought it a shame to keep so much knowledge to myself.

SIR OLIVER. [Aside.] Mercy upon me! learning that had run in the family like an heirloom!—[Aloud.] Pray, what are become of the books?

CHARLES. You must inquire of the auctioneer, Master Premium, for I don't believe even Moses can direct you.

MOSES. I know nothing of books.

SIR OLIVER. So, so, nothing of the family property left, I suppose?

CHARLES. Not much, indeed; unless you have a mind to the family pictures. I have got a room full of ancestors above; and if you have a taste for old paintings, egad, you shall have 'em a bargain!

SIR OLIVER. Hey! what the devil! sure, you wouldn't sell your forefathers, would you?

CHARLES. Every man of them, to the best bidder.

SIR OLIVER. What! your great-uncles and aunts?

CHARLES. Ay, and my great-grandfathers and grandmothers too.

SIR OLIVER. [Aside.] Now I give him up!—[Aloud.] What the plague, have you no bowels for your own kindred? Odd's life! do you take me for Shylock in the play, that you would raise money of me on your own flesh and blood?

CHARLES. Nay, my little broker, don't be angry: what need you care, if you have your moneys' worth?

SIR OLIVER. Well, I'll be the purchaser: I think I can dispose of the family canvas.—[Aside.] Oh, I'll never forgive him this! never!

[Re-enter CARELESS.]

CARELESS. Come, Charles, what keeps you?

CHARLES. I can't come yet. I'faith, we are going to have a sale above stairs; here's little Premium will buy all my ancestors!

CARELESS. Oh, burn your ancestors!

CHARLES. No, he may do that afterwards, if he pleases. Stay, Careless, we want you: egad, you shall be auctioneer—so come along with us.

CARELESS. Oh, have with you, if that's the case. I can handle a hammer as well as a dice-box! Going! going!

SIR OLIVER. [Aside.] Oh, the profligates!

CHARLES. Come, Moses, you shall be appraiser, if we want one. Gad's life, little Premium, you don't seem to like the business?

SIR OLIVER. Oh yes, I do, vastly! Ha! ha! ha! yes, yes, I think it a rare joke to sell one's family by auction—ha!-ha! [Aside.] Oh, the prodigal!

CHARLES. To be sure! when a man wants money, where the plague should be get assistance, if he can't make free with his own relations!

SIR OLIVER. I'll never forgive him; never! never! [Exeunt.]

## ACT IV

### SCENE I

A Picture Room in CHARLES SURFACE'S House

[Enter CHARLES SURFACE, SIR OLIVER SURFACE, MOSES, and CARELESS.]

CHARLES. Walk in, gentlemen, pray walk in;—here they are, the family of the Surfaces, up to the Conquest.

SIR OLIVER. And, in my opinion, a goodly collection.

CHARLES. Ay, ay, these are done in the true spirit of portrait-painting; no volunteer grace or expression. Not like the works of your modern Raphaels, who give you the strongest resemblance, yet contrive to make your portrait independent of you; so that you may sink the original and not hurt the picture. No, no; the merit of these is the inveterate likeness—all stiff and awkward as the originals, and like nothing in human nature besides.

SIR OLIVER. Ah! we shall never see such figures of men again.

CHARLES. I hope not. Well, you see, Master Premium, what a domestic character I am; here I sit of an evening surrounded by my family. But come, get to your pulpit, Mr. Auctioneer; here's an old gouty chair of my grandfather's will answer the purpose.

CARELESS. Ay, ay, this will do. But, Charles, I haven't a hammers: and what's an auctioneer without his hammer?

CHARLES. Egad, that's true. What parchment have we here? Oh, our genealogy in full. [Taking pedigree down.] Here Careless, you shall have no common bit of mahogany, here's the family tree for you, you rogue! This shall be your hammer, and now you may knock down my ancestors with their own pedigree.

SIR OLIVER. [Aside.] What an unnatural rogue!—an *ex post facto* parricide!

CARELESS. Yes, yes, here's a list of your generation indeed; faith, Charles, this is the most convenient thing you could have found for the business, for 'twill not only serve as a hammer, but a catalogue into the bargain. Come, begin—A-going, a-going, a-going!

CHARLES. Bravo, Careless! Well, here's my great-uncle, Sir Richard Raveline, a marvellous good general in his day, I assure you. He served in all the Duke of Marlborough's wars, and got that cut over his eye at the battle of Malplaquet. What say you, Mr. Premium?

look at him—there's a hero! not cut out of his feathers, as your modern clipped captains are, but enveloped in wig and regimentals, as a general should be. What do you bid?

SIR OLIVER. [Aside to MOSES.] Bid him speak.

MOSES. Mr. Premium would have *you* speak.

CHARLES. Why, then, he shall have him for ten pounds, and I'm sure that's not dear for a staff-officer.

SIR OLIVER. [Aside.] Heaven deliver me! his famous uncle Richard for ten pounds!—[Aloud.] Very well, sir, I take him at that.

CHARLES. Careless, knock down my uncle Richard.—Here, now, is a maiden sister of his, my great-aunt Deborah, done by Kneller, in his best manner and esteemed a very formidable likeness. There she is, you see, a shepherdess feeding her flock. You shall have her for five pounds ten—the sheep are worth the money.

SIR OLIVER. [Aside.] Ah! poor Deborah! a woman who set such a value on herself!—[Aloud.] Five pounds ten—she's mine.

CHARLES. Knock down my aunt Deborah! Here, now, are two that were a sort of cousins of theirs.—You see, Moses, these pictures were done some time ago, when beaux wore wigs, and the ladies their own hair.

SIR OLIVER. Yes, truly, head-dresses appear to have been a little lower in those days.

CHARLES. Well, take that couple for the same.

MOSES. 'Tis a good bargain.

CHARLES. Careless!—This, now, is a grandfather of my mother's, a learned judge, well known on the western circuit.—What do you rate him at, Moses?

MOSES. Four guineas.

CHARLES. Four guineas! Gad's life, you don't bid me the price of his wig.—Mr. Premium, you have more respect for the woolsack; do let us knock his lordship down at fifteen.

SIR OLIVER. By all means.

CARELESS. Gone!

CHARLES. And there are two brothers of his, William and Walter Blunt, Esquires, both members of parliament, and noted speakers; and, what's very extraordinary, I believe, this is the first time they were ever bought or sold.

SIR OLIVER. That is very extraordinary, indeed! I'll take them at your own price, for the honour of parliament.

CARELESS. Well said, little Premium! I'll knock them down at forty.

CHARLES. Here's a jolly fellow—I don't know what relation, but he was mayor of Norwich: take him at eight pounds.

SIR OLIVER. No, no; six pounds will do for the mayor.

CHARLES. Come, make it guineas, and I'll throw you the two aldermen there into the bargain.

SIR OLIVER. They're mine.

CHARLES. Careless, knock down the mayor and aldermen. But, plague on't! we shall be all day retailing in this manner; do let us deal wholesale: what say you, little Premium? Give me three hundred pounds for the rest of the family in the lump.

CARELESS. Ay, ay, that will be the best way.

SIR OLIVER. Well, well, any thing to accommodate you; they are mine. But there is one portrait which you have always passed over.

CARELESS. What, that ill-looking little fellow over the settee!

SIR OLIVER. Yes, sir, I mean that; though I don't think him so ill-looking a little fellow, by any means.

CHARLES. What, that? Oh; that's my uncle Oliver! 'twas done before he went to India.

CARELESS. Your uncle Oliver! Gad, then you'll never be friends, Charles. That, now, to me, is as stern a looking rogue as ever I saw; an unforgiving eye, and a damned disinheriting countenance! an inveterate knave, depend on't. Don't you think so, little Premium?

SIR OLIVER. Upon my soul, sir, I do not; I think it is as honest a looking face as any in the room, dead or alive. But I suppose uncle Oliver goes with the rest of the lumber?

CHARLES. No, hang it! I'll not part with poor Noll. The old fellow has been very good to me, and, egad, I'll keep his picture while I've a room to put it in.

SIR OLIVER. [Aside.] The rogue's my nephew after all!—[Aloud.] But, sir, I have somehow taken a fancy to that picture.

CHARLES. I'm sorry for't, for you certainly will not have it. Oons, haven't you got enough of them?

SIR OLIVER. [Aside.] I forgive him every thing!—[Aloud.] But, sir, when I take a whim in my head, I don't value money. I'll give you as much for that as for all the rest.

CHARLES. Don't tease me, master broker; I tell you I'll not part with it, and there's an end of it.

SIR OLIVER. [Aside.] How like his father the dog is!—[Aloud.] Well, well, I have done.—[Aside.] I did not perceive it before, but I think I never saw such a striking resemblance.—[Aloud.] Here is a draft for your sum.

CHARLES. Why, 'tis for eight hundred pounds!

SIR OLIVER. You will not let Sir Oliver go?

CHARLES. Zounds! no! I tell you, once more.

SIR OLIVER. Then never mind the difference, we'll balance that another time. But give me your hand on the bargain; you are an honest fellow, Charles—I beg pardon, sir, for being so free.—Come, Moses.

CHARLES. Egad, this is a whimsical old fellow!—But hark'ee, Premium, you'll prepare lodgings for these gentlemen.

SIR OLIVER. Yes, yes, I'll send for them in a day or two.

CHARLES. But hold; do now send a genteel conveyance for them, for, I assure you, they were most of them used to ride in their own carriages.

SIR OLIVER. I will, I will—for all but Oliver.

CHARLES. Ay, all but the little nabob.

SIR OLIVER. You're fixed on that?

CHARLES. Peremptorily.

SIR OLIVER. [Aside.] A dear extravagant rogue!—[Aloud.] Good day!—Come, Moses.—[Aside.] Let me hear now who dares call him profligate. [Exit with MOSES.]

CARELESS. Why, this is the oddest genius of the sort I ever met with!

CHARLES. Egad, he's the prince of brokers, I think. I wonder how the devil Moses got acquainted with so honest a fellow.—Ha! here's Rowley.—Do, Careless, say I'll join the company in a few moments.

CARELESS. I will—but don't let that old blockhead persuade you to squander any of that money on old musty debts, or any such nonsense; for tradesmen, Charles, are the most exorbitant fellows.

CHARLES. Very true, and paying them is only encouraging them.

CARELESS. Nothing else.

CHARLES. Ay, ay, never fear.—[Exit CARELESS.] So! this was an odd old fellow, indeed. Let me see, two-thirds of these five hundred and thirty odd pounds are mine by right. 'Fore heaven! I find one's ancestors are more valuable relations than I took them for!—Ladies and gentlemen, your most obedient and very grateful servant. [Bows ceremoniously to the pictures.]

[Enter ROWLEY.]

Ha! old Rowley! egad, you are just come in time to take leave of your old acquaintance.

ROWLEY. Yes, I heard they were a-going. But I wonder you can have such spirits under so many distresses.

CHARLES. Why, there's the point! my distresses are so many, that I can't afford to part with my spirits; but I shall be rich and splenetic, all in good time. However, I suppose you are surprised that I am not more sorrowful at parting with so many near relations; to be sure, 'tis very affecting, but you see they never move a muscle, so why should I?

ROWLEY. There's no making you serious a moment.

CHARLES. Yes, faith, I am so now. Here, my honest Rowley, here, get me this changed directly, and take a hundred pounds of it immediately to old Stanley.

ROWLEY. A hundred pounds! Consider only—

CHARLES. Gad's life, don't talk about it! poor Stanley's wants are pressing, and, if you don't make haste, we shall have some one call that has a better right to the money.

ROWLEY. Ah! there's the point! I never will cease dunning you with the old proverb—

CHARLES. Be just before you're generous.—Why, so I would if I could; but Justice is an old, hobbling beldame, and I can't get her to keep pace with Generosity, for the soul of me.

ROWLEY. Yet, Charles, believe me, one hour's reflection—

CHARLES. Ay, ay, it's very true; but, hark'ee, Rowley, while I have, by Heaven I'll give; so, damn your economy! and now for hazard. [Exeunt.]

## SCENE II

Another room in the same

[Enter SIR OLIVER SURFACE and MOSES.]

MOSES. Well, sir, I think, as Sir Peter said, you have seen Mr. Charles in high glory; 'tis great pity he's so extravagant.
SIR OLIVER. True, but he would not sell my picture.
MOSES. And loves wine and women so much
SIR OLIVER. But he would not sell my picture.
MOSES. And games so deep.
SIR OLIVER. But he would not sell my picture. Oh, here's Rowley.

[Enter ROWLEY.]

ROWLEY. So, Sir Oliver, I find you have made a purchase—
SIR OLIVER. Yes, yes, our young rake has parted with his ancestors like old tapestry.
ROWLEY. And here has he commissioned me to redeliver you part of the purchase money—I mean, though, in your necessitous character of Old Stanley.
MOSES. Ah! there is the pity of all; he is so damned charitable.
ROWLEY. And I left a hosier and two tailors in the hall, who, I'm sure, won't be paid, and this hundred would satisfy them.
SIR OLIVER. Well, well, I'll pay his debts, and his benevolence too. But now I am no more a broker, and you shall introduce me to the elder brother as old Stanley.
ROWLEY. Not yet awhile; Sir Peter, I know, means to call there about this time.

[Enter TRIP.]

TRIP. Oh, gentlemen, I beg pardon for not showing you out; this way—Moses, a word. [Exit with MOSES.]
SIR OLIVER. There's a fellow for you! Would you believe it, that puppy intercepted the Jew on our coming, and wanted to raise money before he got to his master!
ROWLEY. Indeed!
SIR OLIVER. Yes, they are now planning an annuity business. Ah, Master Rowley, in my days servants were content with the follies

of their masters, when they were worn a little threadbare; but now they have their vices, like their birthday clothes, with the gloss on. [Exeunt.]

## SCENE III

A Library in JOSEPH SURFACE'S House

[Enter JOSEPH SURFACE and SERVANT.]

JOSEPH. No letter from Lady Teazle?
SERVANT. No, sir.
JOSEPH. [Aside.] I am surprised she has not sent, if she is prevented from coming. Sir Peter certainly does not suspect me. Yet I wish I may not lose the heiress, through the scrape I have drawn myself into with the wife; however, Charles' imprudence and bad character are great points in my favour. [Knocking without.]
SERVANT. Sir, I believe that must be Lady Teazle.
JOSEPH. Hold! See whether it is or not, before you go to the door: I have a particular message for you if it should be my brother.
SERVANT. 'Tis her ladyship, sir; she always leaves her chair at the milliner's in the next street.
JOSEPH. Stay, stay; draw that screen before the window—that will do;—my opposite neighbour is a maiden lady of so curious a temper—[SERVANT draws the screen, and exit.] I have a difficult hand to play in this affair. Lady Teazle has lately suspected my views on Maria; but she must by no means be let into that secret,—at least, till I have her more in my power.

[Enter LADY TEAZLE.]

LADY TEAZLE. What, sentiment in soliloquy now? Have you been very impatient? O Lud! don't pretend to look grave. I vow I couldn't come before.
JOSEPH. O madam, punctuality is a species of constancy very unfashionable in a lady of quality. [Places chairs, and sits after LADY TEAZLE is seated.]
LADY TEAZLE. Upon my word, you ought to pity me. Do you know Sir Peter is grown so ill-natured to me of late, and so jealous of Charles too—that's the best of the story, isn't it?
JOSEPH. [Aside.] I am glad my scandalous friends keep that up.
LADY TEAZLE. I am sure I wish he would let Maria marry him, and then perhaps he would be convinced; don't you, Mr. Surface?

JOSEPH. [Aside.] Indeed I do not.—[Aloud.] Oh, certainly I do! for then my dear Lady Teazle would also be convinced how wrong her suspicions were of my having any design on the silly girl.

LADY TEAZLE. Well, well, I'm inclined to believe you. But isn't it provoking, to have the most ill-natured things said of one? And there's my friend Lady Sneerwell has circulated I don't know how many scandalous tales of me, and all without any foundation too; that's what vexes me.

JOSEPH. Ay, madam, to be sure, that is the provoking circumstance—without foundation; yes, yes, there's the mortification, indeed; for when a scandalous story is believed against one, there certainly is no comfort like the consciousness of having deserved it.

LADY TEAZLE. No, to be sure, then I'd forgive their malice; but to attack me, who am really so innocent, and who never say an ill-natured thing of any body—that is, of any friend; and then Sir Peter, too, to have him so peevish, and so suspicious, when I know the integrity of my own heart—indeed 'tis monstrous!

JOSEPH. But, my dear Lady Teazle, 'tis your own fault if you suffer it. When a husband entertains a groundless suspicion of his wife, and withdraws his confidence from her, the original compact is broken, and she owes it to the honour of her sex to endeavour to outwit him.

LADY TEAZLE. Indeed! So that, if he suspects me without cause, it follows, that the best way of curing his jealousy is to give him reason for't?

JOSEPH. Undoubtedly—for your husband should never be deceived in you: and in that case it becomes you to be frail in compliment to his discernment.

LADY TEAZLE. To be sure, what you say is very reasonable, and when the consciousness of my innocence—

JOSEPH. Ah, my dear madam, there is the great mistake! 'tis this very conscious innocence that is of the greatest prejudice to you. What is it makes you negligent of forms, and careless of the world's opinion? why, the consciousness of your own innocence. What makes you thoughtless in your conduct, and apt to run into a thousand little imprudences? why, the consciousness of your own innocence. What makes you impatient of Sir Peter's temper, and outrageous at his suspicions? why, the consciousness of your innocence.

LADY TEAZLE. 'Tis very true!

JOSEPH. Now, my dear Lady Teazle, if you would but once make a trifling *faux pas*, you can't conceive how cautious you would grow, and how ready to humour and agree with your husband.

LADY TEAZLE. Do you think so?

JOSEPH. Oh, I am sure on't; and then you would find all scandal would cease at once, for—in short, your character at present is like a person in a plethora, absolutely dying from too much health.

LADY TEAZLE. So, so; then I perceive your prescription is, that I must sin in my own defence, and part with my virtue to preserve my reputation?

JOSEPH. Exactly so, upon my credit, ma'am.

LADY TEAZLE. Well, certainly this is the oddest doctrine, and the newest receipt for avoiding calumny!

JOSEPH. An infallible one, believe me. Prudence, like experience, must be paid for.

LADY TEAZLE. Why, if my understanding were once convinced—

JOSEPH. Oh, certainly, madam, your understanding should be convinced. Yes, yes—Heaven forbid I should persuade you to do any thing you thought wrong. No, no, I have too much honour to desire it.

LADY TEAZLE. Don't you think we may as well leave honour out of the argument? [Rises.]

JOSEPH. Ah, the ill effects of your country education, I see, still remain with you.

LADY TEAZLE. I doubt they do indeed; and I will fairly own to you, that if I could be persuaded to do wrong, it would be by Sir Peter's ill usage sooner than your honourable logic, after all.

JOSEPH. Then, by this hand, which he is unworthy of— [Taking her hand.]

[Re-enter SERVANT.]

'Sdeath, you blockhead—what do you want?

SERVANT. I beg your pardon, sir, but I thought you would not choose Sir Peter to come up without announcing him.

JOSEPH. Sir Peter!—Oons—the devil!

LADY TEAZLE. Sir Peter! O Lud! I'm ruined! I'm ruined!

SERVANT. Sir, 'twasn't I let him in.

LADY TEAZLE. Oh! I'm quite undone! What will become of me? Now, Mr. Logic—Oh! mercy, sir, he's on the stairs—I'll get behind here—and if ever I'm so imprudent again— [Goes behind the screen.]

JOSEPH. Give me that book. [Sits down. SERVANT pretends to adjust his chair.]

[Enter SIR PETER TEAZLE.]

SIR PETER. Ay, ever improving himself—Mr. Surface, Mr. Surface—[Pats JOSEPH on the shoulder.]

JOSEPH. Oh, my dear Sir Peter, I beg your pardon.—[Gaping, throws away the book.] I have been dozing over a stupid book. Well, I am much obliged to you for this call. You haven't been here, I believe, since I fitted up this room. Books, you know, are the only things I am a coxcomb in.

SIR PETER. "Tis very neat indeed. Well, well, that's proper; and you can make even your screen a source of knowledge—hung, I perceive, with maps.

JOSEPH. Oh, yes, I find great use in that screen.

SIR PETER. I dare say you must, certainly, when you want to find any thing in a hurry.

JOSEPH. [Aside.] Ay, or to hide any thing in a hurry either.

SIR PETER. Well, I have a little private business—

JOSEPH. [To SERVANT.] You need not stay.

SERVANT. No, sir. [Exit.]

JOSEPH. Here's a chair, Sir Peter—I beg—

SIR PETER. Well, now we are alone, there is a subject, my dear friend, on which I wish to unburden my mind to you—a point of the greatest moment to my peace; in short, my good friend, Lady Teazle's conduct of late has made me very unhappy.

JOSEPH. Indeed! I am very sorry to hear it.

SIR PETER. 'Tis but too plain she has not the least regard for me; but, what's worse, I have pretty good authority to suppose she has formed an attachment to another.

JOSEPH. Indeed! you astonish me!

SIR PETER. Yes! and, between ourselves, I think I've discovered the person.

JOSEPH. How! you alarm me exceedingly.

SIR PETER. Ay, my dear friend, I knew you would sympathize with me!

JOSEPH. Yes, believe me, Sir Peter, such a discovery would hurt me just as much as it would you.

SIR PETER. I am convinced of it. Ah! it is a happiness to have a friend whom we can trust even with one's family secrets. But have you no guess who I mean?

JOSEPH. I haven't the most distant idea. It can't be Sir Benjamin Backbite!

SIR PETER. Oh no! What say you to Charles?

JOSEPH. My brother! impossible!

SIR PETER. Oh, my dear friend, the goodness of your own heart misleads you. You judge of others by yourself.

JOSEPH. Certainly, Sir Peter, the heart that is conscious of its own integrity is ever slow to credit another's treachery.

SIR PETER. True; but your brother has no sentiment—you never hear him talk so.

JOSEPH. Yet I can't but think Lady Teazle herself has too much principle.

SIR PETER. Ay; but what is principle against the flattery of a handsome, lively young fellow?

JOSEPH. That's very true.

SIR PETER. And then, you know, the difference of our ages makes it very improbable that she should have any great affection for me; and if she were to be frail, and I were to make it public, why the town would only laugh at me, the foolish old bachelor, who had married a girl.

JOSEPH. That's true, to be sure—they would laugh.

SIR PETER. Laugh! ay, and make ballads, and paragraphs, and the devil knows what of me.

JOSEPH. No, you must never make it public.

SIR PETER. But then again—that the nephew of my old friend, Sir Oliver, should be the person to attempt such a wrong, hurts me more nearly.

JOSEPH. Ay, there's the point. When ingratitude barbs the dart of injury, the wound has double danger in it.

SIR PETER. Ay—I, that was, in a manner, left his guardian; in whose house he had been so often entertained; who never in my life denied him—my advice!

JOSEPH. Oh, 'tis not to be credited! There may be a man capable of such baseness, to be sure; but, for my part, till you can give me positive proofs, I cannot but doubt it. However, if it should be proved on him, he is no longer a brother of mine—I disclaim kindred with him: for the man who can break the laws of hospitality, and tempt the wife of his friend, deserves to be branded as the pest of society.

SIR PETER. What a difference there is between you! What noble sentiments!

JOSEPH. Yet I cannot suspect Lady Teazle's honour.

SIR PETER. I am sure I wish to think well of her, and to remove all ground of quarrel between us. She has lately reproached me more than once with having made no settlement on her; and, in our last quarrel, she almost hinted that she should not break her heart if I was dead. Now, as we seem to differ in our ideas of expense, I have resolved she shall have her own way, and be her own mistress in that respect for the future; and, if I were to die, she will find I have not been inattentive to her interest while living. Here, my friend, are the drafts of two deeds, which I wish to have your opinion on. By one, she will enjoy eight hundred a year independent while I live; and, by the other, the bulk of my fortune at my death.

JOSEPH. This conduct, Sir Peter, is indeed truly generous.—[Aside.] I wish it may not corrupt my pupil.

SIR PETER. Yes, I am determined she shall have no cause to complain, though I would have not have her acquainted with the latter instance of my affection yet awhile.

JOSEPH. [Aside.] Nor I, if I could help it.

SIR PETER. And now, my dear friend, if you please, we will talk over the situation of your hopes with Maria.

JOSEPH. [Softly.] Oh, no, Sir Peter; another time, if you please.

SIR PETER. I am sensibly chagrined at the little progress you seem to make in her affections.

JOSEPH. [Softly.] I beg you will not mention it. What are my disappointments when your happiness is in debate!—[Aside.] 'Sdeath, I shall be ruined every way!

SIR PETER. And though you are averse to my acquainting Lady Teazle with your passion, I'm sure she's not your enemy in the affair.

JOSEPH. Pray, Sir Peter, now oblige me. I am really too much affected by the subject we have been speaking of to bestow a thought on my own concerns. The man who is entrusted with his friend's distresses can never—

[Re-enter SERVANT.]

Well, sir?

SERVANT. Your brother, sir, is speaking to a gentleman in the street, and says he knows you are within.

JOSEPH. 'Sdeath, blockhead, I'm not within—I'm out for the day.

SIR PETER. Stay—hold—a thought has struck me:—you shall be at home.

JOSEPH. Well, well, let him come up.—[Exit SERVANT.] [Aside.] He'll interrupt Sir Peter, however.

SIR PETER. Now, my good friend, oblige me, I entreat you. Before Charles comes, let me conceal myself somewhere, then do you tax him on the point we have been talking, and his answer may satisfy me at once.

JOSEPH. Oh, fie, Sir Peter! would you have me join in so mean a trick?—to trepan my brother too?

SIR PETER. Nay, you tell me you are sure he is innocent; if so you do him the greatest service by giving him an opportunity to clear himself, and you will set my heart at rest. Come, you shall not refuse me: [Going up.] here, behind the screen will be—Hey! what the devil! there seems to be one listener here already—I'll swear I saw a petticoat!

JOSEPH. Ha! ha! ha! Well, this is ridiculous enough. I'll tell you, Sir Peter, though I hold a man of intrigue to be a most despicable character, yet, you know, it does not follow that one is to be an absolute Joseph either! Hark'ee, 'tis a little French milliner, a silly rogue that plagues me; and having some character to lose, on your coming, sir, she ran behind the screen.

SIR PETER. Ah, Joseph! Joseph! Did I ever think that you—But, egad, she has overheard all I have been saying of my wife.

JOSEPH. Oh, 'twill never go any farther, you may depend upon it!

SIR PETER. No! then, faith, let her hear it out.—Here's a closet will do as well.

JOSEPH. Well, go in there.

SIR PETER. Sly rogue! sly rogue! [Goes into the closet.]

JOSEPH. A narrow escape, indeed! and a curious situation I'm in, to part man and wife in this manner.

LADY TEAZLE. [Peeping.] Couldn't I steal off?

JOSEPH. Keep close, my angel!

SIR PETER. [Peeping.] Joseph, tax him home.

JOSEPH. Back, my dear friend!

LADY TEAZLE. [Peeping.] Couldn't you lock Sir Peter in?

JOSEPH. Be still, my life!

SIR PETER. [Peeping.] You're sure the little milliner won't blab?

JOSEPH. In, in, my dear Sir Peter!—'Fore Gad, I wish I had a key to the door.

[Enter CHARLES SURFACE.]

CHARLES. Hullo! brother, what has been the matter? Your fellow would not let me up at first. What! have you had a Jew or a wench with you?

JOSEPH. Neither, brother, I assure you.

CHARLES. But what has made Sir Peter steal off? I thought he had been with you.

JOSEPH. He *was*, brother; but, hearing you were coming, he did not choose to stay.

CHARLES. What! was the old gentleman afraid I wanted to borrow money of him?

JOSEPH. No, sir; but I am sorry to find, Charles, you have lately given that worthy man grounds for great uneasiness.

CHARLES. Yes, they tell me I do that to a great many worthy men. But how so, pray?

JOSEPH. To be plain with you, brother, he thinks you are endeavouring to gain Lady Teazle's affections from him.

CHARLES. Who, I? O Lud! not I, upon my word—Ha! ha! ha! so the old fellow has found out that he has got a young wife, has he?—or, what is worse, Lady Teazle has found out she has an old husband?

JOSEPH. This is no subject to jest on, brother. He who can laugh—

CHARLES. True, true, as you were going to say—then, seriously, I never had the least idea of what you charge me with, upon my honour.

JOSEPH. [Raising his voice.] Well, it will give Sir Peter great satisfaction to hear this.

CHARLES. To be sure, I once thought the lady seemed to have taken a fancy to me; but, upon my soul, I never gave her the least encouragement. Besides, you know my attachment to Maria.

JOSEPH. But sure, brother, even if Lady Teazle had betrayed the fondest partiality for you—

CHARLES. Why, look'ee Joseph, I hope I shall never deliberately do a dishonourable action, but if a pretty woman was purposely to throw herself in my way—and that pretty woman married to a man old enough to be her father—

JOSEPH. Well!

CHARLES. Why, I believe I should be obliged to—

JOSEPH. What?

CHARLES. To borrow a little of your morality, that's all. But, brother, do you know now that you surprise me exceedingly, by naming me with Lady Teazle; for i' faith, I always understood you were her favourite.

JOSEPH. Oh, for shame, Charles! This retort is foolish.

CHARLES. Nay, I swear I have seen you exchange such significant glances—

JOSEPH. Nay, nay, sir, this is no jest.

CHARLES. Egad, I'm serious! Don't you remember one day, when I called here—

JOSEPH. Nay, pr'ythee, Charles—

CHARLES. And found you together—

JOSEPH. Zounds, sir, I insist—

CHARLES. And another time when your servant—

JOSEPH. Brother, brother, a word with you!—[Aside.] Gad, I must stop him.

CHARLES. Informed, I say, that—

JOSEPH. Hush! I beg your pardon, but Sir Peter has overheard all we have been saying. I knew you would clear yourself, or I should not have consented.

CHARLES. How, Sir Peter! Where is he?

JOSEPH. Softly, there! [Points to the closet.]

CHARLES. Oh, 'fore Heaven, I'll have him out. Sir Peter, come forth!

JOSEPH. No, no—

CHARLES. I say, Sir Peter, come into court.—[Pulls in SIR PETER.] What my old guardian!—What! turn inquisitor, and take evidence incognito? Oh, fie! Oh, fie!

SIR PETER. Give me your hand, Charles—I believe I have suspected; you wrongfully; but you mustn't be angry with Joseph—'twas my plan!

CHARLES. Indeed!

SIR PETER. But I acquit you. I promise you I don't think near so ill of you as I did: what I have heard has given me great satisfaction.

CHARLES. Egad, then, 'twas lucky you didn't hear any more. Wasn't it, Joseph?

SIR PETER. Ah! you would have retorted on him.

CHARLES. Ah, ay, that was a joke.

SIR PETER. Yes, yes, I know his honour too well.

CHARLES. But you might as well have suspected him as me in this matter, for all that. Mightn't he, Joseph?

SIR PETER. Well, well, I believe you.

JOSEPH. [Aside.] Would they were both out of the room.

SIR PETER. And in future, perhaps, we may not be such strangers.

[Re-enter SERVANT, and whispers JOSEPH SURFACE.]

SERVANT. Lady Sneerwell is below, and says she will come up.

JOSEPH. Lady Sneerwell! Gad's life! she must not come here. [Exit SERVANT.] Gentlemen, I beg pardon—I must wait on you down stairs: here is a person come on particular business.

CHARLES. Well, you can see him in another room. Sir Peter and I have not met a long time, and I have something to say to him.

JOSEPH. [Aside.] They must not be left together.—[Aloud.] I'll send Lady Sneerwell away, and return directly.—[Aside to SIR PETER.] Sir Peter, not a word of the French milliner.

SIR PETER. [Aside to JOSEPH SURFACE.] I! not for the world!—[Exit JOSEPH SURFACE.] Ah, Charles, if you associated more with your brother, one might indeed hope for your reformation. He is a man of sentiment. Well, there is nothing in the world so noble as a man of sentiment. Irony *

CHARLES. Pshaw! he is too moral by half; and so apprehensive of his good name, as he calls it, that I suppose he would as soon let a priest into his house as a wench.

SIR PETER. No, no,—come, come—you wrong him. No, no! Joseph is no rake, but he is no such saint either, in that respect.—[Aside.] I have a great mind to tell him—we should have such a laugh at Joseph.

CHARLES. Oh, hang him! he's a very anchorite, a young hermit!

SIR PETER. Hark'ee—you must not abuse him: he may chance to hear of it again, I promise you.

CHARLES. Why, you won't tell him?

SIR PETER. No—but—this way. [Aside.] Egad, I'll tell him—[Aloud.] Hark'ee—have you mind to have a good laugh at Joseph?

CHARLES. I should like it of all things.

SIR PETER. [Whispers.] Then, i'faith, we will! I'll be quit with him for discovering me. He had a girl with him when I called.

CHARLES. What! Joseph? you jest.

SIR PETER. Hush!—a little French milliner—and the best of the jest is—she's in the room now.

CHARLES. The devil she is!

SIR PETER. Hush! I tell you. [Points to the screen.]

CHARLES. Behind the screen! 'Slife, let's unveil her!

SIR PETER. No, no, he's coming:—you shan't, indeed!

CHARLES. Oh, egad, we'll have a peep at the little milliner!

SIR PETER. Not for the world!—Joseph will never forgive me.

CHARLES. I'll stand by you—

SIR PETER. Odds, here he is! [CHARLES SURFACE throws down the screen.]

[Re-enter JOSEPH SURFACE.]

CHARLES. Lady Teazle, by all that's wonderful.
SIR PETER. Lady Teazle, by all that's damnable!
CHARLES. Sir Peter, this is one of the smartest French milliners I ever saw. Egad, you seem all to have been diverting yourselves here at hide and seek, and I don't see who is out of the secret. Shall I beg your ladyship to inform me? Not a word!—Brother, will you be pleased to explain this matter? What! is Morality dumb too?—Sir Peter, though I found you in the dark, perhaps you are not so now! All mute!—Well—though I can make nothing of the affair, I suppose you perfectly understand one another; so I'll leave you to yourselves.—[Going.] Brother, I'm sorry to find you have given that worthy man grounds for so much uneasiness.—Sir Peter! there's nothing in the world so noble as a man of sentiment! [Exit.]
JOSEPH. Sir Peter—notwithstanding—I confess—that appearances are against me—if you will afford me your patience—I make no doubt—but I shall explain every thing to your satisfaction.
SIR PETER. If you please, sir.
JOSEPH. The fact is, sir, that Lady Teazle, knowing my pretensions to your ward Maria—I say, sir, Lady Teazle, being apprehensive of the jealousy of your temper—and knowing my friendship to the family—she, sir, I say—called here—in order that—I might explain these pretensions—but on your coming—being apprehensive—as I said—of your jealousy—she withdrew—and this, you may depend on it, is the whole truth of the matter.
SIR PETER. A very clear account, upon my word; and I dare swear the lady will vouch for every article of it.
LADY TEAZLE. For not one word of it, Sir Peter!
SIR PETER. How! don't you think it worth while to agree in the lie?
LADY TEAZLE. There is not one syllable of truth in what that gentleman has told you.
SIR PETER. I believe you, upon my soul, ma'am!
JOSEPH. [Aside to LADY TEAZLE.] 'Sdeath, madam, will you betray me?
LADY TEAZLE. Good Mr. Hypocrite, by your leave, I'll speak for myself.
SIR PETER. Ay, let her alone, sir; you'll find she'll make out a better story than you, without prompting.
LADY TEAZLE. Hear me, Sir Peter!—I came here on no matter relating to your ward, and even ignorant of this gentleman's pretensions to her. But I came, seduced by his insidious arguments,

at least to listen to his pretended passion, if not to sacrifice your honour to his baseness.

SIR PETER. Now, I believe thee truth is coming, indeed!

JOSEPH. The woman's mad!

LADY TEAZLE. No, sir; she has recovered her senses and your own arts have furnished her with the means.—Sir Peter, I do not expect you to credit me—but the tenderness you expressed for me, when I am sure you could not think I was a witness to it, has so penetrated to my heart, that had I left the place without the shame of this discovery, my future life should have spoken the sincerity of my gratitude. As for that smooth-tongued hypocrite, who would have seduced the wife of his too credulous friend, while he affected honourable addresses to his war—I behold him now in a light so truly despicable, that I shall never again respect myself for having listened to him. [Exit.]

JOSEPH. Notwithstanding all this, Sir Peter, Heaven knows—

SIR PETER. That you are a villain! and so I leave you to your conscience.

JOSEPH. You are too rash, Sir Peter; you shall hear me. The man who shuts out conviction by refusing to—

SIR PETER. Oh, damn your sentiments! [Exeunt Sir Peter and Joseph Surface, talking.]

## ACT V

### SCENE I

The Library in JOSEPH SURFACE'S House

[Enter JOSEPH SURFACE and SERVANT.]

JOSEPH. Mr. Stanley! and why should you think I would see him? you must know he comes to ask something.

SERVANT. Sir, I should not have let him in, but that Mr. Rowley came to the door with him.

JOSEPH. Pshaw! blockhead! to suppose that I should now be in a temper to receive visits from poor relations!—Well, why don't you show the fellow up?

SERVANT. I will, sir.—Why, sir, it was not my fault that Sir Peter discovered my lady—

JOSEPH. Go, fool!—[Exit SERVANT.] Sure Fortune never played a man of my policy such a trick before! My character with Sir Peter, my hopes with Maria, destroyed in a moment! I'm in a rare humour to listen to other people's distresses! I shan't be able to bestow even a benevolent sentiment on Stanley.—So! here he comes, and Rowley with him. I must try to recover myself, and put a little charity into my face, however. [Exit.]

[Enter SIR OLIVER SURFACE and ROWLEY.]

SIR OLIVER. What! does he avoid us? That was he, was it not?

ROWLEY. It was, sir. But I doubt you are come a little too abruptly. His nerves are so weak, that the sight of a poor relation may be too much for him. I should have gone first to break it to him.

SIR OLIVER. Oh, plague of his nerves! Yet this is he whom Sir Peter extols as a man of the most benevolent way of thinking!

ROWLEY. As to his way of thinking, I cannot pretend to decide; for, to do him justice, he appears to have as much speculative benevolence as any private gentleman in the kingdom, though he is seldom so sensual as to indulge himself in the exercise of it.

SIR OLIVER. Yet he has a string of charitable sentiments at his fingers' ends.

ROWLEY. Or, rather, at his tongue's end, Sir Oliver; for I believe there is no sentiment he has such faith in as that Charity begins at home.

SIR OLIVER. And his, I presume, is of that domestic sort which never stirs abroad at all.

ROWLEY. I doubt you'll find it so; but he's coming. I mustn't seem to interrupt you; and you know, immediately as you leave him, I come in to announce your arrival in your real character.

SIR OLIVER. True; and afterwards you'll meet me at Sir Peter's.

ROWLEY. Without losing a moment. [Exit.]

SIR OLIVER. I don't like the complaisance of his features.

[Re-enter JOSEPH SURFACE.]

JOSEPH. Sir, I beg you ten thousand pardons for keeping you a moment waiting.—Mr. Stanley, I presume.

SIR OLIVER. At your service.

JOSEPH. Sir, I beg you will do me the honour to sit down—I entreat you, sir.

SIR OLIVER. Dear sir—there's no occasion.—[Aside.] Too civil by half!

JOSEPH. I have not the pleasure of knowing you, Mr. Stanley; but I am extremely happy to see you look so well. You were nearly related to my mother, I think, Mr. Stanley?

SIR OLIVER. I was, sir; so nearly that my present poverty, I fear, may do discredit to her wealthy children, else I should not have presumed to trouble you.

JOSEPH. Dear sir, there needs no apology;—he that is in distress, though a stranger, has a right to claim kindred with the wealthy. I am sure I wish I was one of that class, and had it in my power to offer you even a small relief.

SIR OLIVER. If your uncle, Sir Oliver, were here, I should have a friend.

JOSEPH. I wish he was, sir, with all my heart; you should not want an advocate with him, believe me, sir.

SIR OLIVER. I should not need one—my distresses would recommend me. But I imagined his bounty would enable you to become the agent of his charity.

JOSEPH. My dear sir, you were strangely misinformed. Sir Oliver is a worthy man, a very worthy man; but avarice, Mr. Stanley, is the vice of age. I will tell you, my good sir, in confidence, what he has done for me has been a mere nothing; though people, I know, have thought otherwise, and for my part, I never chose to contradict the report.

SIR OLIVER. What! has he never transmitted you bullion—rupees—pagodas?

JOSEPH. Oh, dear sir, nothing of the kind! No, no; a few presents now and then—china, shawls, congou tea, avadavats and Indian crackers—little more, believe me.

SIR OLIVER. [Aside.] Here's gratitude for twelve thousand pounds!—Avadavats and Indian crackers!

JOSEPH. Then, my dear sir, you have heard, I doubt not, of the extravagance of my brother: there are very few would credit what I have done for that unfortunate young man.

SIR OLIVER. [Aside.] Not I, for one!

JOSEPH. The sums I have lent him! Indeed I have been exceedingly to blame; it was an amiable weakness; however, I don't pretend to defend it—and now I feel it doubly culpable, since it has deprived me of the pleasure of serving you, Mr. Stanley, as my heart dictates.

SIR OLIVER. [Aside.] Dissembler!—[Aloud.] Then, sir, you can't assist me?

JOSEPH. At present, it grieves me to say, I cannot; but, whenever I have the ability, you may depend upon hearing from me.

SIR OLIVER. I am extremely sorry—

JOSEPH. Not more than I, believe me; to pity, without the power to relieve, is still more painful than to ask and be denied.

SIR OLIVER. Kind sir, your most obedient humble servant.

JOSEPH. You leave me deeply affected, Mr. Stanley.—William, be ready to open the door. [Calls to SERVANT.]

SIR OLIVER. Oh, dear sir, no ceremony.

JOSEPH. Your very obedient.

SIR OLIVER. Your most obsequious.

JOSEPH. You may depend upon hearing from me, whenever I can be of service.

SIR OLIVER. Sweet sir, you are too good!

JOSEPH. In the meantime I wish you health and spirits.

SIR OLIVER. Your ever grateful and perpetual humble servant.

JOSEPH. Sir, yours as sincerely.

SIR OLIVER. [Aside.] Now I am satisfied. [Exit.]

JOSEPH. This is one bad effect of a good character; it invites application from the unfortunate, and there needs no small degree of address to gain the reputation of benevolence without incurring the expense. The silver ore of pure charity is an expensive article in the catalogue of a man's good qualities; whereas the sentimental

French plate I use instead of it makes just as good a show, and pays no tax.

[Re-enter ROWLEY.]

ROWLEY. Mr. Surface, your servant: I was apprehensive of interrupting you, though my business demands immediate attention, as this note will inform you.

JOSEPH. Always happy to see Mr. Rowley,—a rascal.—[Aside. Reads the letter.] Sir Oliver Surface!—My uncle arrived!

ROWLEY. He is, indeed: we have just parted—quite well, after a speedy voyage, and impatient to embrace his worthy nephew.

JOSEPH. I am astonished!—William! stop Mr. Stanley, if he's not gone. [Calls to SERVANT.]

ROWLEY. Oh! he's out of reach, I believe.

JOSEPH. Why did you not let me know this when you came in together?

ROWLEY. I thought you had particular business. But I must be gone to inform your brother, and appoint him here to meet your uncle. He will be with you in a quarter of an hour.

JOSEPH. So he says. Well, I am strangely overjoyed at his coming.—[Aside.] Never, to be sure, was anything so damned unlucky!

ROWLEY. You will be delighted to see how well he looks.

JOSEPH. Oh! I'm overjoyed to hear it.—[Aside.] Just at this time!

ROWLEY. I'll tell him how impatiently you expect him.

JOSEPH. Do, do; pray give my best duty and affection. Indeed, I cannot express the sensations I feel at the thought of seeing him.—[Exit ROWLEY.] Certainly his coming just at this time is the cruellest piece of ill fortune. [Exit.]

## SCENE II

A Room in SIR PETER TEAZLE'S House

[Enter MRS. CANDOUR and Maid.]

MAID. Indeed, ma'am, my lady will see nobody at present.
MRS. CANDOUR. Did you tell her it was her friend Mrs. Candour?
MAID. Yes, ma'am; but she begs you will excuse her.
MRS. CANDOUR. Do go again; I shall be glad to see her, if it be only for a moment, for I am sure she must be in great distress.—[Exit MAID.] Dear heart, how provoking! I'm not mistress of half the circumstances! We shall have the whole affair in the newspapers, with the names of the parties at length, before I have dropped the story at a dozen houses.

[Enter SIR BENJAMIN BACKBITE.]

Oh, dear Sir Benjamin! you have heard, I suppose—
SIR BENJAMIN. Of Lady Teazle and Mr. Surface—
MRS. CANDOUR. And Sir Peter's discovery—
SIR BENJAMIN. Oh, the strangest piece of business, to be sure!
MRS. CANDOUR. Well, I never was so surprised in my life. I am so sorry for all parties, indeed.
SIR BENJAMIN. Now, I don't pity Sir Peter at all: he was so extravagantly partial to Mr. Surface.
MRS. CANDOUR. Mr. Surface! Why, 'twas with Charles Lady Teazle was detected.
SIR BENJAMIN. No, no, I tell you: Mr. Surface is the gallant.
MRS. CANDOUR. No such thing! Charles is the man. 'Twas Mr. Surface brought Sir Peter on purpose to discover them.
SIR BENJAMIN. I tell you I had it from one—
MRS. CANDOUR. And I have it from one—
SIR BENJAMIN. Who had it from one, who had it—
MRS. CANDOUR. From one immediately. But here comes Lady Sneerwell; perhaps she knows the whole affair.

[Enter LADY SNEERWELL.]

LADY SNEERWELL. So, my dear Mrs. Candour, here's a sad affair of our friend Lady Teazle!

MRS. CANDOUR. Ay, my dear friend, who would have thought—

LADY SNEERWELL. Well, there is no trusting appearances; though, indeed, she was always too lively for me.

MRS. CANDOUR. To be sure, her manners were a little too free; but then she was so young!

LADY SNEERWELL. And had, indeed, some good qualities.

MRS. CANDOUR. So she had, indeed. But have you heard the particulars?

LADY SNEERWELL. No; but every body says that Mr. Surface—

SIR BENJAMIN. Ay, there; I told you Mr. Surface was the man.

MRS. CANDOUR. No, no: indeed the assignation was with Charles.

LADY SNEERWELL. With Charles! You alarm me, Mrs. Candour!

MRS. CANDOUR. Yes, yes; he was the lover. Mr. Surface, to do him justice, was only the informer.

SIR BENJAMIN. Well, I'll not dispute with you, Mrs. Candour; but, be it which it may, I hope that Sir Peter's wound will not—

MRS. CANDOUR. Sir Peter's wound! Oh, mercy! I didn't hear a word of their fighting.

LADY SNEERWELL. Nor I, a syllable.

SIR BENJAMIN. No! what, no mention of the duel?

MRS. CANDOUR. Not a word.

SIR BENJAMIN. Oh, yes: they fought before they left the room.

LADY SNEERWELL. Pray, let us hear.

MRS. CANDOUR. Ay, do oblige us with the duel.

SIR BENJAMIN. Sir, says Sir Peter, immediately after the discovery, you are a most ungrateful fellow.

MRS. CANDOUR. Ay, to Charles—

SIR BENJAMIN. No, no—to Mr. Surface—a most ungrateful fellow; and old as I am, sir, says he, I insist on immediate satisfaction.

MRS. CANDOUR. Ay, that must have been to Charles; for 'tis very unlikely Mr. Surface should fight in his own house.

SIR BENJAMIN. Gad's life, ma'am, not at all—giving me immediate satisfaction.—On this, ma'am, Lady Teazle, seeing Sir Peter in such danger, ran out of the room in strong hysterics, and Charles after her, calling out for hartshorn and water; then, madam, they began to fight with swords—

elaborate - moving further away from truth
scandal story

[Enter CRABTREE.]

CRABTREE. With pistols, nephew, pistols! I have it from undoubted authority.

MRS. CANDOUR. Oh, Mr. Crabtree, then it is all true!

CRABTREE. Too true, indeed, madam, and Sir Peter is dangerously wounded—

SIR BENJAMIN. By a thrust in seconde quite through his left side—

CRABTREE. By a bullet lodged in the thorax.

MRS. CANDOUR. Mercy on me! Poor Sir Peter!

CRABTREE. Yes, madam; though Charles would have avoided the matter, if he could.

MRS. CANDOUR. I told you who it was; I knew Charles was the person.

SIR BENJAMIN. My uncle, I see, knows nothing of the matter.

CRABTREE. But Sir Peter taxed him with basest ingratitude—

SIR BENJAMIN. That I told you, you know—

CRABTREE. Do, nephew, let me speak!—and insisted on immediate—

SIR BENJAMIN. Just as I said—

CRABTREE. Odd's life, nephew, allow others to know something too! A pair of pistols lay on the bureau (for Mr. Surface, it seems, had come home the night before late from Salthill, where he had been to see the Montem with a friend, who has a son at Eton), so, unluckily, the pistols were left charged.

SIR BENJAMIN. I heard nothing of this.

CRABTREE. Sir Peter forced Charles to take one, and they fired, it seems, pretty nearly together. Charles' shot took effect, as I tell you, and Sir Peter's missed; but, what is very extraordinary, the ball struck against a little bronze Shakespeare that stood over the fire place, grazed out of the window at a right angle, and wounded the postman, who was just coming to the door with a double letter from Northamptonshire.

SIR BENJAMIN. My uncle's account is more circumstantial, I confess; but I believe mine is the true one, for all that.

LADY SNEERWELL. [Aside.] I am more interested in this affair than they imagine, and must have better information. [Exit.]

SIR BENJAMIN. Ah! Lady Sneerwell's alarm is very easily accounted for.

CRABTREE. Yes, yes, they certainly do say—but that's neither here nor there.

MRS. CANDOUR. But, pray, where is Sir Peter at present?

CRABTREE. Oh! they brought him home, and he is now in the house, though the servants are ordered to deny it.

MRS. CANDOUR. I believe so, and Lady Teazle, I suppose, attending him.

CRABTREE. Yes, yes; and I saw one of the faculty enter just before me.

SIR BENJAMIN. Hey! who comes here?

CRABTREE. Oh, this is he: the physician, depend on't.

MRS. CANDOUR. Oh, certainly! it must be the physician; and now we shall know.

[Enter SIR OLIVER SURFACE.]

CRABTREE. Well, doctor, what hopes?

MRS. CANDOUR. Ay, doctor, how's your patient?

SIR BENJAMIN. Now, doctor, isn't it a wound with a small sword?

CRABTREE. A bullet lodged in the thorax, for a hundred!

SIR OLIVER. Doctor! a wound with a small-sword! and a bullet in the thorax!—Oons! are you mad, good people?

SIR BENJAMIN. Perhaps, sir, you are not a doctor?

SIR OLIVER. Truly, I am to thank you for my degree, if I am.

CRABTREE. Only a friend of Sir Peter's, then, I presume. But, sir, you must have heard of his accident?

SIR OLIVER. Not a word!

CRABTREE. Not of his being dangerously wounded?

SIR OLIVER. The devil he is!

SIR BENJAMIN. Run through the body—

CRABTREE. Shot in the breast—

SIR BENJAMIN. By one Mr. Surface—

CRABTREE. Ay, the younger.

SIR OLIVER. Hey! what the plague! you seem to differ strangely in your accounts: however, you agree that Sir Peter is dangerously wounded.

SIR BENJAMIN. Oh, yes, we agree in that.

CRABTREE. Yes, yes, I believe there can be no doubt of that.

SIR OLIVER. Then, upon my word, for a person in that situation, he is the most imprudent man alive; for here he comes, walking as if nothing at all was the matter.

[Enter SIR PETER TEAZLE.]

Odd's heart, Sir Peter! you are come in good time, I promise you; for we had just given you over!

SIR BENJAMIN. [Aside to CRABTREE.] Egad, uncle, this is the most sudden recovery!

SIR OLIVER. Why, man! what do you out of bed with a small-sword through your body, and a bullet logged in your thorax?

SIR PETER. A small-sword and a bullet!

SIR OLIVER. Ay; these gentlemen would have killed you without law or physic, and wanted to dub me a doctor, to make me an accomplice.

SIR PETER. Why, what is all this?

SIR BENJAMIN. We rejoice, Sir Peter, that the story of the duel is not true, and are sincerely sorry for your other misfortune.

SIR PETER. [Aside.] So, so; all over the town already!

CRABTREE. Though, Sir Peter, you were certainly vastly to blame to marry at your years.

SIR PETER. Sir, what business is that of yours?

MRS. CANDOUR. Though, indeed, as Sir Peter made so good a husband, he's very much to be pitied.

SIR PETER. Plague on your pity, ma'am! I desire none of it.

SIR BENJAMIN. However, Sir Peter, you must not mind the laughing and jests you will meet with on the occasion.

SIR PETER. Sir, sir! I desire to be master in my own house.

CRABTREE. 'Tis no uncommon case, that's one comfort.

SIR PETER. I insist on being left to myself: without ceremony, I insist on your leaving my house directly!

MRS. CANDOUR. Well, well, we are going; and depend on't, we'll make the best report of it we can. [Exit.]

SIR PETER. Leave my house!

CRABTREE. And tell how hardly you've been treated. [Exit.]

SIR PETER. Leave my house!

SIR BENJAMIN. And how patiently you bear it. [Exit.]

SIR PETER. Fiends! vipers! furies! Oh! that their own venom would choke them!

SIR OLIVER. They are very provoking indeed, Sir Peter.

[Enter ROWLEY.]

ROWLEY. I heard high words: what has ruffled you, sir?

SIR PETER. Pshaw! what signifies asking? Do I ever pass a day without my vexations?

ROWLEY. Well, I'm not inquisitive.

SIR OLIVER. Well, Sir Peter, I have seen both my nephews in the manner we proposed.

SIR PETER. A precious couple they are!

ROWLEY. Yes, and Sir Oliver is convinced that your judgment was right, Sir Peter.

SIR OLIVER. Yes, I find Joseph is indeed the man, after all.

ROWLEY. Ay, as Sir Peter says, he is a man of sentiment.

SIR OLIVER. And acts up to the sentiments he professes.

ROWLEY. It certainly is edification to hear him talk.

SIR OLIVER. Oh, he's a model for the young men of the age!—but how's this, Sir Peter? you don't join us in your friend Joseph's praise, as I expected.

SIR PETER. Sir Oliver, we live in a damned wicked world, and the fewer we praise the better.

ROWLEY. What! do you say so, Sir Peter, who were never mistaken in your life?

SIR PETER. Pshaw! plague on you both! I see by your sneering you have heard the whole affair. I shall go mad among you!

ROWLEY. Then, to fret you no longer, Sir Peter, we are indeed acquainted with it all. I met Lady Teazle coming from Mr. Surface's so humbled, that she deigned to request me to be her advocate with you.

SIR PETER. And does Sir Oliver know all this?

SIR OLIVER. Every circumstance.

SIR PETER. What, of the closet and the screen, hey?

SIR OLIVER. Yes, yes, and the little French milliner. Oh, I have been vastly diverted with the story! ha! ha! ha!

SIR PETER. 'Twas very pleasant.

SIR OLIVER. I never laughed more in my life, I assure you: ha! ha! ha!

SIR PETER. Oh, vastly diverting! ha! ha! ha!

ROWLEY. To be sure, Joseph with his sentiments! ha! ha! ha!

SIR PETER. Yes, yes, his sentiments! ha! ha! ha! Hypocritical villain!

SIR OLIVER. Ay, and that rogue Charles to pull Sir Peter out of the closet: ha! ha! ha!

SIR PETER. Ha! ha! 'twas devilish entertaining, to be sure!

SIR OLIVER. Ha! ha! ha! Egad, Sir Peter, I should like to have seen your face when the screen was thrown down: ha! ha!

SIR PETER. Yes, yes, my face when the screen was thrown down: ha! ha! ha! Oh, I must never show my head again!

SIR OLIVER. But come, come, it isn't fair to laugh at you neither, my old friend; though, upon my soul, I can't help it.

SIR PETER. Oh, pray don't restrain your mirth on my account: it does not hurt me at all! I laugh at the whole affair myself. Yes, yes, I think being a standing jest for all one's acquaintance a very happy situation. Oh, yes, and then of a morning to read the paragraphs about Mr. S——, Lady T——, and Sir P——, will be so entertaining!

ROWLEY. Without affectation, Sir Peter, you may despise the ridicule of fools. But I see Lady Teazle going towards the next room; I am sure you must desire a reconciliation as earnestly as she does.

SIR OLIVER. Perhaps my being here prevents her coming to you. Well, I'll leave honest Rowley to mediate between you; but he must bring you all presently to Mr. Surface's, where I am now returning, if not to reclaim a libertine, at least to expose hypocrisy.

SIR PETER. I'll be present at your discovering yourself there with all my heart; though 'tis a vile unlucky place for discoveries.

ROWLEY. We'll follow. [Exit SIR OLIVER SURFACE.]

SIR PETER. She is not coming here, you see, Rowley.

ROWLEY. No, but she has left the door of that room open, you perceive. See, she is in tears.

SIR PETER. Certainly a little mortification appears very becoming in a wife. Don't you think it will do her good to let her pine a little?

ROWLEY. Oh, this is ungenerous in you!

SIR PETER. Well, I know not what to think. You remember the letter I found to hers evidently intended for Charles?

ROWLEY. A mere forgery, Sir Peter! laid in your way on purpose. This is one of the points which I intend Snake shall give you conviction of.

SIR PETER. I wish I were once satisfied of that. She looks this way. What a remarkably elegant turn of the head she has! Rowley, I'll go to her.

ROWLEY. Certainly.

SIR PETER. Though, when it is known that we are reconciled, people will laugh at me ten times more.

ROWLEY. Let them laugh, and retort their malice only by showing them you are happy in spite of it.

SIR PETER. I' faith, so I will! and, if I'm not mistaken, we may yet be the happiest couple in the country.

ROWLEY. Nay, Sir Peter, he who once lays aside suspicion—

SIR PETER. Hold, Master Rowley! if you have any regard for me, never let me hear you utter any thing like a sentiment: I have had enough of them to serve me the rest of my life. [Exeunt.]

reconciled himself — he will make up with ~~them~~ Lady Teazle

## SCENE III

The Library of JOSEPH SURFACE'S House

[Enter JOSEPH SURFACE and LADY SNEERWELL.]

LADY SNEERWELL. Impossible! Will not Sir Peter immediately be reconciled to Charles, and of course no longer oppose his union with Maria? The thought is distraction to me.

JOSEPH. Can passion furnish a Remedy?

LADY SNEERWELL. No, nor cunning either. Oh, I was a fool, an idiot, to league with such a blunderer!

JOSEPH. Sure, Lady Sneerwell, I am the greatest sufferer; yet you see I bear the accident with calmness.

LADY SNEERWELL. Because the disappointment doesn't reach your heart; your interest only attached you to Maria. Had you felt for her what I have for that ungrateful libertine, neither your temper nor hypocrisy could prevent your showing the sharpness of your vexation.

JOSEPH. But why should you reproaches fall on me for this disappointment?

LADY SNEERWELL. Are you not the cause of it? Had you not a sufficient field for your roguery in imposing upon Sir Peter, and supplanting your brother, but you must endeavour to seduce his wife? I hate such an avarice of crimes; 'tis an unfair monopoly, and never prospers.

JOSEPH. Well, I admit I have been to blame. I confess I deviated from the direct road of wrong, but I don't think we're so totally defeated neither.

LADY SNEERWELL. No!

JOSEPH. You tell me you have made a trial of Snake since we met, and that you still believe him faithful to us?

LADY SNEERWELL. I do believe so.

JOSEPH. And that he has undertaken, should it be necessary, to swear and prove that Charles is at this time contracted by vows and honour to your ladyship—which some of his former letters to you will serve to support.

LADY SNEERWELL. This, indeed, might have assisted.

JOSEPH. Come, come; it is not too late yet.—[Knocking at the door.] But hark! this is probably my uncle, Sir Oliver: retire to that room; we'll consult farther when he is gone.

LADY SNEERWELL. Well, but if he should find you out too?

JOSEPH. Oh, I have no fear of that. Sir Peter will hold his tongue for his own credit's sake—and you may depend on it I shall soon discover Sir Oliver's weak side!

LADY SNEERWELL. I have no diffidence of your abilities: only be constant to one roguery at a time.

JOSEPH. I will, I will!—[Exit LADY SNEERWELL.] So! 'tis confounded hard, after such bad fortune, to be baited by one's confederate in evil. Well, at all events, my character is so much better than Charles', that I certainly—hey!—what—this is not Sir Oliver, but old Stanley again. Plague on't that he should return to tease me just now! I shall have Sir Oliver come and find him here—and—

[Enter SIR OLIVER SURFACE.]

Gad's life, Mr. Stanley, why have you come back to plague me at this time? You must not stay now, upon my word.

SIR OLIVER. Sir, I hear your uncle Oliver is expected here, and though he has been so penurious to you, I'll try what he'll do for me.

JOSEPH. Sir, 'tis impossible for you to stay now, so I must beg—Come any other time, and I promise you, you shall be assisted.

SIR OLIVER. No: Sir Oliver and I must be acquainted.

JOSEPH. Zounds, sir! then I insist on your quitting the room directly.

SIR OLIVER. Nay, sir—

JOSEPH. Sir, I insist on't—Here, William! show this gentleman out. Since you compel me, sir, not one moment—this is such insolence. [Going to push him out.]

[Enter CHARLES SURFACE.]

CHARLES. Heyday! what's the matter now? What the devil, have you got hold of my little broker here? Zounds, brother, don't hurt little Premium. What's the matter, my little fellow?

JOSEPH. So! he has been with you too, has he?

CHARLES. To be sure, he has. Why, he's as honest a little—But sure, Joseph, you have not been borrowing money too, have you?

JOSEPH. Borrowing! no! But, brother, you know we expect Sir Oliver here every—

CHARLES. O Gad, that's true! Noll mustn't find the little broker here, to be sure.

JOSEPH. Yet Mr. Stanley insists—

CHARLES. Stanley! why his name's Premium.

JOSEPH. No, sir, Stanley.

CHARLES. No, no, Premium.

JOSEPH. Well, no matter which—but—

CHARLES. Ay, ay, Stanley or Premium, 'tis the same thing, as you say; for I suppose he goes by half a hundred names, besides A. B. at the coffee-house. [Knocking.]

JOSEPH. 'Sdeath! here's Sir Oliver at the door.—Now I beg, Mr. Stanley—

CHARLES. Ay, ay, and I beg, Mr. Premium—

SIR OLIVER. Gentlemen—

JOSEPH. Sir, by Heaven you shall go!

CHARLES. Ay, out with him, certainly!

SIR OLIVER. This violence—

JOSEPH. Sir, 'tis your own fault.

CHARLES. Out with him, to be sure. [Both forcing SIR OLIVER out.

[Enter SIR PETER and LADY TEAZLE, MARIA, and ROWLEY.]

SIR PETER. My old friend, Sir Oliver—hey! What in the name of wonder—here are dutiful nephews—assault their uncle at a first visit!

LADY TEAZLE. Indeed, Sir Oliver, 'twas well we came in to rescue you.

ROWLEY. Truly it was; for I perceive, Sir Oliver, the character of old Stanley was no protection to you.

SIR OLIVER. Nor of Premium either: the necessities of the former could not extort a shilling from that benevolent gentleman; and with the other I stood a chance of faring worse than my ancestors, and being knocked down without being bid for.

JOSEPH. Charles!

CHARLES. Joseph!

JOSEPH. 'Tis now complete!

CHARLES. Very.

SIR OLIVER. Sir Peter, my friend, and Rowley too—look on that elder nephew of mine, You know what he has already received from my bounty; and you also know how gladly I would have regarded half my fortune as held in trust for him: judge then my disappointment in discovering him to be destitute of truth, charity, and gratitude!

SIR PETER. Sir Oliver, I should be more surprised at this declaration, if I had not myself found him to be mean, treacherous, and hypocritical.

LADY TEAZLE. And if the gentleman pleads not guilty to these, pray let him call *me* to his character.

SIR PETER. Then, I believe, we need add no more: if he knows himself, he will consider it as the most perfect punishment, that he is known to the world.

CHARLES. [Aside.] If they talk this way to Honesty, what will they say to me, by and by? [SIR PETER, LADY TEAZLE, and MARIA retire.]

SIR OLIVER. As for that prodigal, his brother, there—

CHARLES. [Aside.] Ay, now comes my turn: the damned family pictures will ruin me!

JOSEPH. Sir Oliver—uncle, will you honour me with a hearing?

CHARLES. [Aside.] Now, if Joseph would make one of his long speeches I might recollect myself a little.

SIR OLIVER. [To JOSEPH SURFACE.] I suppose you would undertake to justify yourself?

JOSEPH. I trust I could.

SIR OLIVER. [To CHARLES SURFACE.] Well, sir!—and you could justify yourself too, I suppose?

CHARLES. Not that I know of, Sir Oliver.

SIR OLIVER. What!—Little Premium has been let too much into the secret, I suppose?

CHARLES. True, sir; but they were family secrets, and should not be mentioned again, you know.

ROWLEY. Come, Sir Oliver, I know you cannot speak of Charles' follies with anger.

SIR OLIVER. Odd's heart, no more I can; nor with gravity either. Sir Peter, do you know the rogue bargained with me for all his ancestors; sold me judges and generals by the foot, and maiden aunts as cheap as broken china.

CHARLES. To be sure, Sir Oliver, I did make a little free with the family canvas, that's the truth on't. My ancestors may rise in judgment against me, there's no denying it; but believe me sincere when I tell you—and upon my soul I would not say so if I was not—that if I do not appear mortified at the exposure of my follies, it is because I feel at this moment the warmest satisfaction in seeing you, my liberal benefactor.

SIR OLIVER. Charles, I believe you, Give me your hand again: the ill-looking little fellow over the settee has made your peace.

CHARLES. Then, sir, my gratitude to the original is still increased.

LADY TEAZLE. [Advancing.] Yet, I believe, Sir Oliver, here is one Charles is still more anxious to be reconciled to. [Pointing to MARIA.]

SIR OLIVER. Oh, I have heard of his attachment there; and, with the young lady's pardon, if I construe right—that blush—

SIR PETER. Well, child, speak your sentiments!

MARIA. Sir, I have little to say, but that I shall rejoice to hear that he is happy; for me, whatever claim I had to his attention, I willingly resign to one who has a better title.

CHARLES. How, Maria!

SIR PETER. Heyday! what's the mystery now? While he appeared an incorrigible rake, you would give your hand to no one else; and now that he is likely to reform I'll warrant you won't have him!

MARIA. His own heart and Lady Sneerwell know the cause.

CHARLES. Lady Sneerwell!

JOSEPH. Brother, it is with great concern I am obliged to speak on this point, but my regard to justice compels me, and Lady Sneerwell's injuries can no longer be concealed. [Opens the door.]

[Enter LADY SNEERWELL.]

SIR PETER. So! another French milliner! Egad, he has one in every room in the house, I suppose!

LADY SNEERWELL. Ungrateful Charles! Well may you be surprised, and feel for the indelicate situation your perfidy has forced me into.

CHARLES. Pray, uncle, is this another plot of yours? For, as I have life, I don't understand it.

JOSEPH. I believe, sir, there is but the evidence of one person more necessary to make it extremely clear.

SIR PETER. And that person, I imagine, is Mr. Snake.—Rowley, you were perfectly right to bring him with us, and pray let him appear.

ROWLEY. Walk in, Mr. Snake.

[Enter SNAKE.]

I thought his testimony might be wanted: however, it happens unluckily, that he comes to confront Lady Sneerwell, not to support her.

LADY SNEERWELL. A villain! Treacherous to me at last! Speak, fellow, have you too conspired against me?

SNAKE. I beg your ladyship ten thousand pardons: you paid me extremely liberally for the lie in question; but I unfortunately have been offered double to speak the truth.

SIR PETER. Plot and counter-plot, egad! I wish your ladyship joy of your negotiation.

LADY SNEERWELL. The torments of shame and disappointment on you all! [Going.]

LADY TEAZLE. Hold, Lady Sneerwell—before you go, let me thank you for the trouble you and that gentleman have taken, in writing letters from me to Charles, and answering them yourself; and let me also request you to make my respects to the scandalous college of which you are president, and inform them that Lady Teazle, licentiate, begs leave to return the diploma they granted her, as she leaves off practice, and kills characters no longer.

LADY SNEERWELL. You too, madam!—provoking—insolent! May your husband live these fifty years! [Exit.]

SIR PETER. Oons! what a fury!

LADY TEAZLE. A malicious creature, indeed!

SIR PETER. What! not for her last wish?

LADY TEAZLE. Oh, no!

SIR OLIVER. Well, sir, and what have you to say now?

JOSEPH. Sir. I am so confounded, to find that Lady Sneerwell could be guilty of suborning Mr. Snake in this manner, to impose on us all, that I know not what to say: however, lest her revengeful spirit should prompt her to injure my brother, I had certainly better follow her directly. For the man who attempts to—[Exit.]

SIR PETER. Moral to the last!

SIR OLIVER. Ay, and marry her, Joseph, if you can. Oil and vinegar!—egad you'll do very well together.

ROWLEY. I believe we have no more occasion for Mr. Snake at present?

SNAKE. Before I go, I beg pardon once for all, for whatever uneasiness I have been the humble instrument of causing to the parties present.

SIR PETER. Well, well, you have made atonement by a good deed at last.

SNAKE. But I must request of the company, that it shall never be known.

SIR PETER. Hey! what the plague! are you ashamed of having done a right thing once in your life?

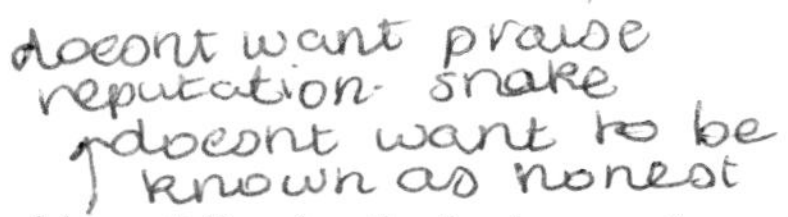




SNAKE. Ah, sir, consider—I live by the badness of my character; and, if it were once known that I had been betrayed into an honest action, I should lose every friend I have in the world.

SIR OLIVER. Well, well—we'll not traduce you by saying any thing in your praise, never fear. [Exit SNAKE.]

SIR PETER. There's a precious rogue!

LADY TEAZLE. See, Sir Oliver, there needs no persuasion now to reconcile your nephew and Maria,

SIR OLIVER. Ay, ay, that's as it should be, and, egad, we'll have the wedding to-morrow morning.

CHARLES. Thank you, dear uncle.

SIR PETER. What, you rogue! don't you ask the girls consent first?

CHARLES. Oh, I have done that a long time—a minute ago—and she has looked *yes*.

MARIA. For shame, Charles!—I protest, Sir Peter, there has not been a word—

SIR OLIVER. Well, then, the fewer the better; may your love for each other never know abatement.

SIR PETER. And may you live as happily together as Lady Teazle and I intend to do!

CHARLES. Rowley, my old friend, I am sure you congratulate me; and I suspect that I owe you much.

SIR OLIVER. You do, indeed, Charles.

SIR PETER. Ay, honest Rowley always said you would reform.

CHARLES. Why, as to reforming, Sir Peter, I'll make no promises, and that I take to be a proof that I intend to set about it. But here shall be my monitor—my gentle guide.—Ah! can I leave the virtuous path those eyes illumine?

Though thou, dear maid, shouldst waive thy beauty's sway,
Thou still must rule, because I will obey:
An humble fugitive from Folly view,
No sanctuary near but Love and you:

[To the Audience.]

You can, indeed, each anxious fear remove,
For even Scandal dies, if you approve.

[Exeunt omnes.]

## EPILOGUE

By MR. COLMAN;
Spoken by LADY TEAZLE

I, who was late so volatile and gay,
Like a trade-wind must now blow all one way,
Bend all my cares, my studies, and my vows,
To one dull rusty weathercock—my spouse!
So wills our virtuous bard—the motley Bayes
Of crying epilogues and laughing plays!
Old bachelors, who marry smart young wives,
Learn from our play to regulate your lives:
Each bring his dear to town, all faults upon her—
London will prove the very source of honour.
Plunged fairly in, like a cold bath it serves,
When principles relax, to brace the nerves:
Such is my case; and yet I must deplore
That the gay dream of dissipation 's o'er.
And say, ye fair! was ever lively wife,
Born with a genius for the highest life,
Like me untimely blasted in her bloom,
Like me condemn'd to such a dismal doom?
Save money—when I just knew how to waste it!
Leave London—just as I began to taste it!
Must I then watch the early crowing cock,
The melancholy ticking of a clock;
In a lone rustic hall for ever pounded,
With dogs, cats, rats, and squalling brats surrounded?
With humble curate can I now retire.
(While good Sir Peter boozes with the squire)
And at backgammon mortify my soul,
That pants for loo, or flutters at a vole?
'Seven's the main!' Dear sound that must expire,
Lost at hot cockles round a Christmas fire;
The transient hour of fashion too soon spent,
Farewell the tranquil mind, farewell content!
Farewell the plumèd head, the cushioned *tête*,
That takes the cushion from its proper seat!
That spirit—stirring drum!—card drums I mean,
Spadille—odd trick—pam—basto—king and queen!